C000292306

55 Ways to Connect with Families in your Parish

Karen Kent

VERITAS

Published 2017 by
Veritas Publications
7–8 Lower Abbey Street
Dublin 1, Ireland
publications@veritas.ie
www.veritas.ie

ISBN 978 1 84730 801 6
Copyright © Karen Kent, 2017

Prayers taken or adapted from: *The Family Prayer Book*, Dublin:
Veritas, 2012 (p. 67); Bishop Kevin Manning, Diocese of Parramatta,
Australia (p. 111); *The Veritas Book of Blessing Prayers*, Dublin: Veritas,
1989 (p. 122); Canadian Catholic Bishops' Conference, *Blessings and
Prayers for the Home and Family*, ACTA Publications, 2008 (pp. 141,
143); www.thischurch.com – St Mark's Church, Bedford.

10 9 8 7 6 5 4 3 2 1

The material in this publication is protected by copyright law. Except
as may be permitted by law, no part of the material may be reproduced
(including by storage in a retrieval system) or transmitted in any
form or by any means, adapted, rented or lent without the written
permission of the copyright owners. Applications for permissions
should be addressed to the publisher.

A catalogue record for this book is available from the British Library.

Cover design by Heather Costello, Veritas Publications
Printed in the Republic of Ireland by SPRINT-print Ltd, Dublin

The royalties from this publication are kindly donated to Cork and
Ross Pastoral Development Office to further their work of catechesis
with families.

*Veritas books are printed on paper made from the wood pulp of managed
forests. For every tree felled, at least one tree is planted, thereby renewing
natural resources.*

CONTENTS

Introduction 9

ADVENT

1. Las Posadas: The Journey to Bethlehem 17
2. Advent Wreath: Lighting the Candles 20
3. The Jesse Tree: Tracing the Family Tree of Jesus 27
4. Advent Candle. 33
5. Bambinelli Sunday 34
6. Advent Giving Tree of Love 36
7. Saint Nicholas: Letters to Father Christmas 38

CHRISTMAS

8. Preparing our Parish Crib 42
9. Procession to the Crib 44
10. Celebrating Babies Born in our Parish this Year 45
11. A Gift of Christmas Dinner 47
12. Happy Christmas to One and All! 48
13. Crib Walk. 50
14. Holy Family: Blessing of Families 52
15. Epiphany: the Journey of the Magi 54
16. Epiphany: Celebrating all Nations 56

LENT, HOLY WEEK AND EASTER

17. Ash Wednesday . . . . ·59
18. Lenten Family Prayer Space. 64
19. Lenten Blessings Box 67
20. Fast – Pray – Give 70
21. The Cross of Hope . . . . ·72
22. Family Stations of the Cross. ·73
23. Holy Thursday: Newly Blessed Oils. 75
24. Easter Sunday: Easter Egg Hunt . . . . ·78

FEAST DAYS

25. Baptism of the Lord: Celebrating the Newly Baptised . . . 83
26. Saint Brigid: Making and Blessing the Cross 86
27. Saint Valentine: Celebrating Love and Marriage 90
28. Saint Patrick: Praying for Emigrants. 93
29. Saint Anthony: Blessing of Lilies for the Sick. 95
30. Pentecost: Celebrating all Nations. 98
31. Saints Joachim and Anne: Celebrating Grandparents . . 101
32. Saint Francis: Blessing of Pets and Animals. 103

THROUGH THE YEAR

33. Mother's Day and Father's Day 107
34. November, We Remember 110
35. Send a Card. 112
36. Preparing for Baptism 114
37. Celebrating with those Confirmed 116
38. Praying for those Sitting Exams 119
39. Ice-Cream Sunday. 121

40. Family Rosary 123

41. Offertory Procession............................124

42. Blessing of the School Bags 126

43. First Day at School 129

44. Visitation of Families for First Holy Communion 130

45. A Snapshot of Parish Life: World Photography Day . . 132

46. The Act of Giving: World Homeless Day 134

47. Parish Picnic 135

48. Family Prayer Pack 137

49. Blessing of Homes 138

50. Blessing of Expectant Parents 140

51. Children's Liturgy Group: Sharing the Word of God . . 142

52. Pancake Party 144

53. World Book Day: Storytelling. 146

54. Family Meals Together 147

55. Celebrating the Talent in our Parish 150

APPENDIX FOR PARISHES IN IRELAND

56. Grow in Love: Prayer Services 152

57. Catholic Schools Week 154

INTRODUCTION

Why connect with families in the parish? How will we connect with families in our parish?

This book of ideas is the fruit of twelve years of ministry in parishes in the Diocese of Cork and Ross, includes reflection on my own formation in the faith, from growing up in England to joining the Ursuline Sisters in Ireland. Every step of my life journey has had some bearing on the gathering of these ideas together, from childhood memories of the crib walk during the Christmas holidays to receiving cards from my home parish on the anniversary of my profession, my birthday, Christmas and Easter every year since I joined the Ursulines. These cards are reminders to me that people continue to pray for me as I journey through life.

As an Ursuline sister I joined a long tradition of women inspired by the vision of Angela Merici, who, between the 1480s and 1535, responded personally to the needs of her time and place as she witnessed the war, the destruction of her hometown in Italy and the breakdown in family life. She saw the need for catechesis in the heart of the homes of Brescia and in the minds and hearts of families, as she herself had experienced as a child.

It was this need that led her to found the Company of Saint Ursula, consecrated women who would live a life committed to Gospel values in the heart of their own family or in their place of work in service to the large Brescian households of the time. The context for Angela was always the home and the family in their local community. Her guiding principle was that each person would be known 'not only by their name but also their condition, and character, and their very situation and state' (*Second Legacy*). This, she says, will not be difficult if we embrace them with ardent charity. Through this she hoped that each person would know themselves as loved by God and that Christ would be the centre of every home and family.

So, as we respond to Pope Francis and his teaching to us in *Amoris Laetitia* (*The Joy of Love*), I see Angela Merici's words and thoughts echoed once again today. As we look at our parishes today and hear the words of Pope Francis who says to us that '[the parish] continues to be "the Church living in the midst of the homes of her sons and daughters" (*Christifideles Laici*, 26). This presumes that it really is in contact with the homes and lives of its people' (*Evangelii Gaudium*, 28).

In these words I hear an echo of Saint Angela speaking to the leaders of her newly formed company, 'Go often, as you have time and opportunity ... and visit your dear daughters and sisters, and greet them; see how they are, comfort them; encourage them to stand fast in the life begun' (*Fifth Counsel*). To be in contact and to see how people are requires visitation. I offer here ideas for meeting with parents of children preparing for the sacraments. Visiting and meeting with parents and the wider family helps reconnect them with the local faith community and encourages the handing on of the faith. In these meetings the parishioner comes as Christ the visitor, who we meet throughout the Gospels calling to the homes of friends, neighbours and strangers to extend the merciful love of God to them.

Every parish is called on by Pope Francis to take opportunities as they arise to go forth, to be missionaries in their time and place, to connect, to greet, to bring God's love through small gestures of kindness and compassion. This book seeks to offer small initiatives that local parishes can take on to come together to celebrate family, to rejoice in our faith, to show love and to meet Christ in one another.

I hope every reader will see something here that will help their parish to take the first steps in reaching out to share with the 'coming generation the glorious deeds of the Lord' (*AL*, 16) as together we go forth to care for others and seek their happiness (cf. *AL*, 324). Let us take this opportunity as we journey together towards hosting the World Meeting of Families in Ireland in 2018 to 'leave a mark on the life of others' (*AL*, 322) by the joy of our love, celebrated and shared with all whom we encounter.

How to use this book
The fifty-five ideas in this book are intended as a menu from which a parish pastoral leadership group can select. Just as one chooses from a restaurant menu to suit one's taste so one chooses from this selection according to the particular parish and its people.

The menu here offers catechetical, liturgical and ecclesial moments that will lead parishioners of all ages to a closer relationship with Christ, the Church and one another. The catechetical moments are based around family time – and families come in all shapes and sizes, so it is intended that most of the ideas can include all households in your parish community. Everyone belongs to a family and all who are baptised are members of God's family into which they were 'welcomed with great joy' on the day of their Baptism, according to the baptismal rite.

So it is for each parish pastoral leadership group to seek to live these moments of connection with joy in the local community we call parish, which is where people experience Church together. No parish is expected to do everything and all of the ideas can be adapted to suit the needs of time and place.

So as you discern how to connect with families, think of those who come to your Church regularly, those who come occasionally and those who have become somewhat disconnected. The door is open to all people to come and share in the love of Jesus Christ. Look at the ideas offered here and decide what would fit best in your parish. Through prayer and discussion, the right ideas for connecting will present themselves to you as you journey through the year – and remember each year you can try something different from the menu.

As you will see, some of the ideas are connected to the liturgical year in the Church, while others take their lead from the secular calendar. The latter can be brought into our faith context, allowing them to speak to us of Christ and offering us opportunities to connect with the secular celebrations in our society today.

For each idea presented here I have given the necessary texts of prayers, readings and stories, alongside practical suggestions for how to make them work in your parish. At the beginning of each idea I have offered a scripture quotation. I invite those who use this book to take a moment to reflect on these words so that this does not become merely an instruction manual. The end of each idea offers a quotation from the recent apostolic exhortation on love in the family, *Amoris Laetitia*, gifted to us by Pope Francis in 2016. These short quotations will, I hope, encourage deeper engagement with this text from the Holy Father. In *Amoris Laetita*, Pope Francis shares his reflections following the two synods on the family with the whole world. He invites us to 'keep striving towards something greater than ourselves and our families ... that fullness of love and communion which God holds out before us' (325).

More information about Saint Angela Merici and the Ursuline sisters can be found at: www.ursulines.ie.

ADVENT

1. LAS POSADAS:
THE JOURNEY TO BETHLEHEM

Joseph set out from the town of Nazareth in Galilee for
Judaea, to David's town called Bethlehem ... to be
registered with Mary, his betrothed, who was with child
(Lk 2:4–5)

Las Posadas (meaning 'the inns') is a Mexican tradition that we can borrow to help families in our parishes engage with the journey of Mary and Joseph to Bethlehem. Traditionally the Mexican people celebrate Las Posadas from 16 to 24 December. You may choose to follow this eight day tradition; however, to allow more families to participate you can start your journey at the beginning of Advent.

In early November begin to ask for host families who will offer a ready welcome to Mary and Joseph as they make their way to Bethlehem to participate in the census called by Emperor Augustus. Travelling through the parish, Mary and Joseph carry with them a diary that each family is invited to fill in each day of their stay – so creating your own parish story of their journey. They also carry with them a story card of the journey to Bethlehem and the nativity of Jesus that each host family reads together as Mary and Joseph come to stay at their 'inn'.

Many of our parishes have large crib figures which are not suitable for this activity; however, one easy way to overcome this is to invite the knitters of the parish to knit three figures – Mary, Joseph and the donkey – for you to use in your parish Posada.

During Advent, beginning on the First Sunday, Mary and Joseph travel from house to house and families are asked to care for them during their stay with them. The figures can become the focus of conversation in the home, be part of bedtime stories and have a special place created for them in the home. Before handing the figures on to the next 'innkeepers', the host family are asked to fill in the diary of the journey and record their stay at their home – who they met, what they enjoyed as part of their visit.

On Christmas Eve the last host family brings the figures to the church for the Vigil Mass.

Story card (Lk 2:1–5)

In those days a decree went out from Emperor Augustus that all the world should be registered. This was the first registration and was taken while Quirinius was governor of Syria. All went to their own town to be registered. Joseph also went from the town of Nazareth in Galilee to Judea, to the city of David called Bethlehem, because he was descended from the house and family of David. He went to be registered with Mary, to whom he was engaged and who was expecting a child.

FAMILY PRAYER

In my heart, Mary and Joseph, I will journey with you and others for Las Posadas. In our homes we joyfully share in your journey, dear Mary and Joseph, as you make your way to Bethlehem. It is there that your holy child will be born in a borrowed stable and then we will feast and sing and rejoice. The long, hard journey has ended. Your newborn child will bring us so much joy this Christmas.

If you have an excess of volunteer innkeepers, you could also make a set of Magi figures with their gifts of gold, frankincense and myrrh, who also make a journey in your parish. Set them off on the Third Sunday of Advent also carrying their story card and their diary to record their journey. They arrive at the church on the Feast of Epiphany (6 January) at the Vigil Mass.

Children need symbols, actions and stories
(AL, 288)

2. ADVENT WREATH: LIGHTING THE CANDLES

Prepare a way for the Lord
(Mk 1:3)

On each of the four Sundays of Advent we light a candle on the Advent wreath in our churches and on Christmas Day we light the fifth candle. Each Sunday invite a different family to come forward to light the candle. 'Family' here may include grandparents, parents and children together. Inviting the family forward is part of our engagement and encouragement of families in our liturgies. Often we invite an individual, yet there are times such as this when families can participate together.

On each Sunday invite a different family to participate. At the beginning of Mass invite them forward. One of them lights the candle while another gives the introduction to the theme of the week. Then together they pray the prayer for the particular Sunday.

FIRST SUNDAY OF ADVENT
Purple candle – The candle of hope
Today we remember the ancestors of Jesus.

FAMILY MEMBER: Today is the First Sunday of Advent, in which we recall the hope we have in Christ. God told Abraham that through him all the nations of the world would be blessed, because he trusted and put his hope in God. The Old Testament spoke of the coming of Christ, of how a saviour would be born, a king in the line of King David. He would rule the world wisely and bless all the nations. We too believe in God's promise to send Jesus again to this world to establish his kingdom upon the earth.

A family member lights the first candle – the candle of hope.

Hope is like a light shining in a dark place. As we look at the light of this candle we celebrate the hope we have in Jesus Christ.

FAMILY MEMBER: Let us pray. God of Abraham and Sarah and all the patriarchs of old, you are our Father too. Your love is revealed to us in Jesus Christ, Son of God, and Son of David. Help us in preparing to celebrate his birth, to make our hearts ready and to place our hope in you. Help us today and every day to worship you, to hear your word, and to do your will by sharing your hope with others. We ask this in the name of the one who was born in Bethlehem. Amen.

SECOND SUNDAY OF ADVENT
Purple candle – the candle of peace
Today we remember the prophets who foretold the birth of Christ.

FAMILY MEMBER: Today is the Second Sunday of Advent and we will light the candle of peace. We remember the prophets who spoke of the coming of Christ, of how a saviour would be born, a king in the line of King David. The prophet Isaiah called Christ 'the Prince of Peace'. He told us how he would rule the world wisely and bless all the nations.

When Jesus came he taught people the importance of being peacemakers. He said that those who make peace shall be called the children of God. When Christ comes to us he brings us peace and he will bring everlasting peace when he comes again. We light the candle of peace to remind us that Jesus is the Prince of Peace and that through him peace is found.

A family member lights the second candle – the candle of peace.

Peace is like a light shining in a dark place. As we look at this candle we celebrate the peace we find in Jesus Christ.

FAMILY MEMBER: Let us pray. Lord Jesus, Light of the World, the prophets said you would bring peace and save your people from trouble. Give peace in our hearts at Christmastide. We ask this as we wait for you to come again, that you remain present with us. Help us today and every day to worship you, to hear your word, and to do your will by sharing your peace with each other. We ask this in the name of the one who was born in Bethlehem. Amen.

THIRD SUNDAY OF ADVENT
Pink candle – the candle of joy

FAMILY MEMBER: Today we light the third candle of Advent, the candle of joy. When the angel Gabriel told Mary that a special child would be born to her she was filled with joy. She sang a song that began with the words: 'My soul magnifies the Lord, my spirit rejoices in God my Saviour.' Just as the birth of Jesus gave great joy to his mother, so his presence in the world gave joy to those who had none before. He healed them and gave them hope and peace when they believed in him.

We light the candle of joy to remind us that when Jesus is born in us we have joy and that through him there will be everlasting joy on earth.

A family member lights the third candle – the candle of joy.

Joy is like a light shining in a dark place. As we look at this candle we celebrate the joy we find in Jesus Christ.

FAMILY MEMBER: Let us pray. Thank you God for the joy you give us. We ask that as we wait for all your promises to come true, and for Christ to come again, that you remain present with us. Help us today and every day to worship you, to hear your word and to do your will by sharing your joy with each other. We ask this in the name of the one who was born in Bethlehem. Amen.

FOURTH SUNDAY OF ADVENT

Purple candle – the candle of love

Today we remember John the Baptist who prepared the way for the coming of Christ.

FAMILY MEMBER: Today we light the third candle of Advent, the candle of love. In their old age, God gave to Zechariah and Elizabeth a son called John. John spoke to the people bravely in the desert, denying his own comforts and prepared to die for what he believed. John taught that we should share what we have with others, treat each other kindly and show God's love. He did this because he cared for people and wanted them to repent and find God's forgiveness.

A family member lights the third candle – the candle of love.

Love is like a candle shining in a dark place. As we look at the light of this candle we celebrate the love we have in Christ.

FAMILY MEMBER: Let us pray. Lord God, your witness John the Baptist grew up strong in spirit and prepared people for the coming of the Lord. He loved your people and baptised them in the River Jordan to wash away their sins. Help us to have the same love, that we may be witnesses to him and spread the good news of your love. As Christmas draws closer day by day, help us to be ready to welcome him with love. Amen.

CHRISTMAS DAY
White candle – the birth of Jesus Christ

FAMILY MEMBER: Today is Christmas Day, in which we recall the hope we have in Christ. Today we light again the candles of hope, peace, joy and love.

A family member lights each candle in turn as the reader speaks.

First candle: We speak of hope – because God keeps his promises to us.

Second candle: We work for peace – because Jesus is the 'Prince of Peace' and he calls his children to work for peace in his name.

Third candle: We share joy – because the Holy Spirit fills our hearts and minds with the presence the God.

Fourth candle: We show love – because Jesus gave everything for us and led us to know the forgiveness of God.

White candle (Christmas Day): Now we light our last candle to remember the birth of our Lord and Saviour Jesus Christ. As the prophets promised so long ago, you have come to us once again; and with the shepherds, we are filled with wonder and amazement.

Lord, you come as a tiny, fragile baby, yet we know that you are God and you are with us. May the flame of this candle remind us that you are the Light of the World and that if we follow you, we will never walk in darkness, but will have the true light of life. Lord Jesus we welcome you into our midst. Amen.

By their witness as well as their words, families speak to others of Jesus. They pass on the faith, they arouse a desire for God and they reflect the beauty of the Gospel and its way of life
(AL, 184)

3. THE JESSE TREE: TRACING THE FAMILY TREE OF JESUS

An account of the genealogy of Jesus the Messiah
(Mt 1:1)

Firstly, you need a good-sized tree that can be placed in the sanctuary or other significant place in the church. On Christmas Eve the tree can then be placed near the crib so that people can see the tracing of the family tree of Jesus as they visit the crib. It could be a standard fir that is used as a Christmas tree.

Invite children from the parish to come together to make and colour the symbols for the Jesse Tree. These will help all the parishioners to trace the family origins of Jesus and the story that led to his birth at Christmas time.

Alternatively, you could ask four different families to take the templates, colour them in, and then come forward at the beginning of the Mass to hang the four symbols for that week on the Jesse Tree. The parents could give the explanation of the symbols as their children hang them on the tree.

SYMBOLS AND STORY
WEEK ONE
Adam and Eve (Gn 3:1–24)   **Apple**
The symbol of the apple is chosen to represent the forbidden fruit that Adam and Eve ate from the tree in the Garden of Eden in disobedience to God's command.

Noah and the flood (Gn 6:13–9:17) **Rainbow and dove**
The story of Noah and the flood shows God's faithfulness to his people. Noah trusted God, doing as he was asked, and, therefore, he, his family and all the animals were saved. The rainbow is the symbol of God's covenant (his promise) to his people, while the dove is the promise of peace for all of God's creation.

Abraham, the father of God's people (Gn 16:1–6)
Figure of Abraham and star
Abraham was a descendent of Noah and the first great leader of God's people. He always showed faith and trust in God's promises. As Abraham looked to the sky at the number of stars, too many too count, he knew that God would keep his promise to him that he would have many descendants who would be God's holy people, because with God all things are possible.

The sacrifice of Isaac (Gn 22:1–18) **Dagger**
Abraham demonstrated his total love for God by his willingness to sacrifice his precious son. God rewarded this faithfulness by at the last moment giving Abraham an alternative sacrifice of a ram.

WEEK TWO
Jacob's ladder (Gn 28:10–22) **Ladder**
In his dream, Jacob (son of Isaac) saw a ladder reaching from earth to heaven, indicating to him that God would always protect and care for him and his descendants, giving them a special name as the 'people of Israel'.

Joseph feeds God's people (Gn 41:37–45)   Wheat sheaves
Joseph (favourite son of Jacob) experienced his brothers plotting against him but God constantly protected him from harm. Joseph, in turn, stayed close to God, never seeking revenge against his brothers or misusing the power given to him by Pharaoh. Instead, he forgave those who sought to harm him and ensured that all the children of Israel had food to eat and did not suffer.

Moses leads the people out of Egypt (Ex 14:10–31)   Staff
Moses was another of the great leaders of the people of Israel, who, at God's command, defied Pharaoh and led the people from slavery in Egypt to the Promised Land. He did this because he trusted in God. He used his staff to make a path through the sea so that his people could pass through safely.

Moses receives the Ten Commandments (Ex 20:1–17)
Stone tablet
God gave to Moses these Ten Commandments that would allow the people of Israel to live their lives close to him and in peace and harmony with one another.

WEEK THREE
Isaiah's prophecy (Is 11:1–2)   Scroll
Isaiah was one of the prophets, someone who sees things according to God's plans and speaks in the name of God with words given by God. Isaiah, having been called by God in a vision in the temple, came to understand that salvation lies in complete faith and trust in God. He foretold the coming of the true son of David, the saviour who would bring peace and

love to the world. The scroll symbolises the fulfilment of the prophecy of Isaiah.

Bethlehem house (1 Sm 16:4–13)   House

Jesse was a descendant of Abraham, who lived in Bethlehem. God had chosen Jesse's youngest son, David, to be the successor of King Saul and lead the people of Israel. God promised that he would send a saviour who would be a descendant of Jesse's family and come from Bethlehem, their home – hence the symbol of the home.

King David the harpist (1 Sm 16:14–23)   Harp

David is the youngest son of Jesse, who God chose to lead his people. He is known as the psalmist who wrote many of the psalms in the Old Testament. He united the people and brought the Ark of the Covenant to Jerusalem and made plans to build a Temple there. He is symbolised by his harp.

King Solomon (1 Kgs 3:16–28)   Crown

Solomon was David's son and is known for his wise sayings. Under his leadership the people of Israel enjoyed peace and prosperity. He continued the building of the Temple as his father had planned. Here the people worshipped and it became central to the life of Israel.

WEEK FOUR

Joseph the carpenter (Mt 1:18–25)   Hammer and saw

Joseph, like his ancestors, had great faith and trust in God and so when Mary, to whom he was betrothed, announced she was to have a baby, he did as God asked and took her as his wife. Joseph took on the responsibilities of fatherhood for Jesus, taking care of him and Mary. He shared fully in the early earthly life of Jesus and probably taught Jesus his own trade of carpentry.

Mary the Mother of Jesus (Lk 1:26–38)   rose

At the annunciation, Mary learned from God that she had been chosen as mother of his son, the promised saviour. To God's request she responded with faith and trust, confident that with God all things are possible. Mary is represented by a white rose, a flower which represents purity and perfection.

John the Baptist (Lk 1:57–80)

Writing tablet with 'His name is John' inscribed

John the Baptist was the son of Elizabeth and Zechariah, a gift to them from God. At the announcement of his birth, Zechariah was struck dumb and had to write the child's name down when asked. He wrote, 'His name is John'. This was against the tradition of naming a child after the family. John was filled with the Holy Spirit from his birth and was the one who prepared the way for Jesus, the promised Messiah.

Jesus the Messiah (Mt 1:25; 2:9–11)   Star

Jesus, the promised saviour, was born in Bethlehem, the city of David, in a place marked by the star seen by the wise men when they came to visit.

If you have four families preparing your parish Jesse Tree, ask the parents to prepare the story as they would tell it to their children. Otherwise, invite a parishioner to write the story to be told each week, based on the biblical text and the short explanation given here after each symbol.

Help children to realise they are part of an age-old
pilgrimage and that they need to
respect all that came before them
(AL, 192)

4. ADVENT CANDLE

The people that walked in darkness have seen a great light
(Is 9:2)

Introduce the idea of a candle in the homes of your parish for
Advent. Make Advent candles available either as a gift or for
parishioners to buy for a small charge. Families are invited
to light their candle together each day of Advent and to say
the Advent family prayer together. Provide a prayer card with
every candle.

This idea is for all age groups. Everyone belongs to a family,
whatever their daily living situation, so ensure that those who
live alone also feel included!

ADVENT FAMILY PRAYER
God of Love, your son, Jesus, is your greatest gift to us.
He is a sign of your love. As we light our Advent candle
may it remind us of the love you have for us.
Help us to walk in that love during the weeks of Advent,
as we wait and prepare for his coming. We pray in the
name of Jesus, our saviour. Amen.

This is something you could also make available to the sick
and the housebound of the parish, giving them a candle too
so they can join in with the parish at prayer.

Every family ... can become a light in the darkness
of the world
(AL, 66)

5. BAMBINELLI SUNDAY

While they were there, the time came for her to deliver her
child. And she gave birth to her firstborn son and wrapped
him in bands of cloth and laid him in a manger
(Lk 2:6-7)

Gaudete Sunday is the third Sunday of Advent. *Gaudete* means 'rejoice' and so on this day we rejoice that Christ is coming. Each year the pope invites families (children and adults) to bring their baby Jesus figure from their family crib to St Peter's Square, where he blesses them during the Angelus.

In your parish you can invite families to bring their baby Jesus figure to Mass with them for the blessing. The family then takes their figure home, puts it in a gift box, wraps it in Christmas paper and places it under the Christmas tree. On Christmas morning this is the first gift the family opens together. They then place the figure into the crib in their home.

BLESSING OF THE BABY JESUS CRIB FIGURES – THE BAMBINELLI

God our Father, you loved us so much you sent us your only son, Jesus, born of the Virgin Mary, to save us and lead us back to you.

We pray that, with your blessing, these images of Jesus might be a sign of your presence and love in our homes. Gracious God, give your blessing to all who will gather with us this Christmas, family and friends.

Open our hearts, that we might receive Jesus in joy, do always what he asks of us and see him in those who need our love.

We ask this in the name of Jesus, your beloved son, who came to give peace to the world. You who live and reign forever and ever. Amen.

The incarnation of the Word in a human family, in Nazareth, by its very newness changed the history of the world
(AL, 65)

6. ADVENT GIVING TREE OF LOVE

Opening their treasure chests, they offered him gifts
(Mt 2:11)

On the first Sunday of Advent have a basket of Christmas gift labels prepared and, as part of the homily, introduce the Giving Tree to the congregation, inviting families to take a gift label home with them from Mass. Have people stationed with a basket at the church doors after Mass, allowing parishioners to take a gift label if they wish.

They are asked to buy a gift for an adult or a child and write on the label whether it is for an adult, stating male or female, or child, stating age group and gender.

Bring your parish Christmas tree into the church for the third Sunday of Advent, but rather than decorating it leave it bare of any ornaments or lights. As part of the offertory of the Mass, invite families to bring their gift and leave it under the tree.

Over the next two weeks arrange with the St Vincent de Paul Society (or another social service or community group) to deliver the gifts to families.

In some parishes it works better to invite parishioners to bring food items that can be distributed to families for the Christmas period, rather than other types of gifts. You will need to decide locally what best suits your situation.

This is a great way to live out the Christmas message of giving of the greatest gift – the gift of love!

The experience of love in families is a perennial source of strength for the life of the Church

(AL, 88)

7. SAINT NICHOLAS: LETTERS TO FATHER CHRISTMAS

The Lord has sent me to bring good news to the poor
(Lk 4:18)

On 6 December we celebrate the feast day of the original Father Christmas, St Nicholas, who was bishop of Smyrna in the sixth century.

In your newsletter on the preceding Sunday tell the story of St Nicholas and invite the children to come to the church on the feast day with their letter to Father Christmas. Have a postbox or bag ready to receive the letters. As part of the homily tell the story of St Nicholas again and invite the children to bring forward their letters and place them in the postbox or bag.

At the end of Mass invite a parishioner to come and take the letters for posting to Father Christmas. This could be a way to get the local postman or postwoman involved.

As people leave the church, distribute small oranges as a reminder of the story of today's feast. The orange came to represent the gift of gold that St Nicholas dropped down the chimney into the house.

Story of St Nicholas

There was a poor man who had three daughters. He was so poor, he did not have enough money for a dowry so his daughters couldn't get married. The dowry was a gift given by the girl's father to her new husband on their marriage. Without it one could not get married.

One night, Nicholas secretly dropped a bag of gold down the chimney and into the house. This meant that the oldest daughter was able to be married. The bag fell into a stocking that had been hung by the fire to dry! This was repeated later with the second daughter. Finally, determined to discover the person who had given him the money, the father secretly hid by the fire every evening until he caught Nicholas dropping in a bag of gold. Nicholas begged the man not to tell anyone what he had done, because he did not want to bring attention to himself. But soon the news got out and when anyone received a secret gift, it was thought that it was from Nicholas.

It is this story that leads us to see St Nicholas as the forerunner to Father Christmas and why we leave stockings by the fire on Christmas Eve, in the hope of a visit from Father Christmas with presents for us. The traditional stocking gifts of the orange and the gold coins (today usually of the chocolate kind!) to symbolise the gifts St Nicholas dropped down the chimney into the stockings. Because of his kindness Nicholas was made a saint.

This is an opportunity to invite parents and grandparents to come with the pre-school children to Mass or even to invite junior and senior infant classes to Mass – you could also invite their parents and grandparents to join.

Open and caring families find a place for the poor and build friendships with those less fortunate than themselves
(AL, 183)

CHRISTMAS

8. PREPARING OUR PARISH CRIB

Make it live again in our time, make it known in our time
(Hab 3:2)

In all of our parishes we have cribs in our churches, and often outside our churches to allow the true message of Christmas to shine forth in our world.

Setting up the figures is a favourite activity of children. Why not invite a different family (or perhaps an extended family of grandparents, parents, children, cousins, aunts and uncles) each year to assist in the setting up of the crib in your church. You could invite two or three families to work together, or families from the same street, neighbourhood, townland. Be creative in your local setting and make this work as well as possible for your parish.

Allow the children to choose where the figures will be placed in the space created. Let them use their imagination in setting up the crib, even if it differs from the usual scene.

While the children set out the figures in preparation for Christmas Eve, give the parents the story card to read with their children.

Story card (Lk 2:6–14)

Now it happened while they were there, the time came for her to have her child, and she gave birth to a son, her firstborn. She wrapped him in swaddling clothes and laid him in a manger because there was no room for them at the inn. In the countryside close by there were shepherds out in the fields keeping guard over their sheep during the watches of the night. An angel of the Lord stood over them and the glory of the Lord shone around them. They were terrified, but the angel said, 'Do not be afraid. Look I bring you news of great joy, a joy to be shared by the whole people. Today in the town of David a saviour has been born to you; he is Christ the Lord. And here is a sign for you: you will find a baby wrapped in swaddling clothes and lying in a manger.' And all at once with the angel there was a great throng of the hosts of heaven, praising God with the words:

Glory to God in the highest heaven,
And on earth peace for those he favours.

FAMILY PRAYER

Lord Jesus, you came in the silence of the night,
an extraordinary gift to ordinary people.
Help us to see the wonderful things
you are doing in the ordinary experiences of our lives.
In your name we pray. Amen.

The Church is a family of families, constantly enriched by the lives of all those domestic churches

(AL, 87)

9. PROCESSION TO THE CRIB

*Let us go to Bethlehem and see this event which the Lord
has made known to us*
(Lk 2:15)

At the opening procession of the Vigil Mass of Christmas it
is tradition to go to the crib in the church, bringing the figure
of the child Jesus and blessing the crib before proceeding to
the sanctuary for the beginning of Mass.

This year, why not expand the participation in this
procession. If you have celebrated Las Posadas in your
parish, invite the families who were the innkeepers to join in
the procession. If not, invite a family – parents, children and
grandparents – to bring the child Jesus to the crib.

BLESSING OF THE CRIB

Loving God, we thank you for gathering us here together
to celebrate once again your birth.
Bless this our parish crib which we have prepared,
may it be a reminder to us of your gift to us of Jesus,
your Son,
born of Mary and cared for by Joseph.
We ask your blessing on all who will visit this crib,
just as the shepherds visited you on that first Christmas
night. Amen.

*Nazareth teaches us the meaning of family life, its loving
communion, its simple and austere beauty*
(AL, 66)

10. CELEBRATING BABIES BORN IN OUR PARISH THIS YEAR

May the Lord bless you and keep you.
May the Lord let his face shine upon you
and be gracious to you.
May the Lord show you his face and bring you peace.
(Num 6:24-26)

During Advent, prepare a list of the names of all the babies born or baptised in your parish during the past year. Remember to include babies born in your parish but baptised in another parish. On Christmas Eve, during the opening procession of the Vigil Mass, invite a member of your parish Baptism preparation team to bring to the crib the names of all the babies born or baptised during the past year and leave the names displayed near the crib, thereby celebrating and welcoming all the new members of your parish community.

Alongside the list of names leave a prayer card for those who visit the crib over the Christmas season to pray for all the children who are named and remembered on your parish list this year. Let the families know you are doing this as many would like to come and visit the crib and see their child's name displayed at the crib.

If a baby in your parish was born or baptised during the year and has since died, you might include a special memory of them and their parents at this moment. They can be included in the list with 'RIP' after their name – but it would be respectful to talk to the parents first. Let them decide if they do or do not want to be included. This will take careful handling and great pastoral care for the family involved.

PRAYER FOR OUR CHILDREN

Blessed are you Lord
who gave us the gift of our children.
Be with us as we witness to them our faith in you,
as we read the stories of your life with them
and as we share with them what is means to be brothers
and sisters to all people
that they in their turn will share in the life of your
Church, the family of God. Amen.

The couple that loves and begets life is a true, living icon ...
capable of revealing God the Creator and Saviour
(AL, 11)

11. A GIFT OF CHRISTMAS DINNER

When you have a party invite the poor, the crippled, the
lame and the blind, then you will be blessed
(Lk 14:13–14)

Christmas is often a time of excess food in many homes. This year why not invite families in your parish to gift a Christmas dinner to a person who is living alone, a neighbour or fellow parishioner. Perhaps in your parish or a nearby town there is a charity or a place where Christmas dinner is provided for those who are homeless or have no one with whom to share the Christmas festivities. Families could donate dinners or excess food to these charities, or even volunteer their time over the Christmas period.

Decide how you can best engage in a project such as this in your parish, then during Advent invite parishioners to make a commitment to cook one extra Christmas dinner they will gift to another person. They are asked to invite this person to share the Christmas meal with the family or if the person is housebound, the family might visit and bring the Christmas dinner and spend a little time with them on this special day.

A family's living space could turn into a domestic church, a
setting for the Eucharist,
the presence of Christ seated at its table
(AL, 15)

12. HAPPY CHRISTMAS TO ONE AND ALL!

The whole group of believers was united, heart and soul
(Acts 4:32–35)

Over recent years parish communities have become more multinational and for many newcomers to our cities, towns and villages Christmas can be a time when they think of home and loved ones. As you prepare for the parish Christmas celebrations invite people to share some of the Christmas traditions from their homelands. This can be done through the parish newsletter and website. This simple gesture can help us to get to know each other better. You might even choose to adopt one of these traditions in your parish!

As you prepare for Christmas and are decorating your church include Christmas greetings on banners/signs around the church in the different languages of the people who make up your parish community.

TRANSLATIONS OF 'HAPPY CHRISTMAS'

French:	Joyeux Noel
Portuguese:	Feliz Natal
Polish:	Wesołych Świąt
Arabic:	Miilaad majiid
Spanish:	Feliz Navidad
Italian:	Buon Natale
Slovak:	Vesele vianoce
Latvian:	Priecīgus Ziemassvētkus
Romanian:	Un Crăciun ferici

German:	Fröhliche Weihnachten
Filipino:	Maligayang Pasko!
Chinese:	Tshèng dàn kuài lè
Indonesian:	Selamat Hari Natal
Turkish:	Noeliniz Ve Yeni Yiliniz Kutlu Olsun
Ethiopian:	Melkin Yelidet Beaal
Bosnian:	Čestit Božić I Sretna Nova godina
Swahili:	Kuwa na Krismasi njema

To be open to a genuine encounter with others, a kind look
is essential ... despite our differences
(AL, 100)

13. CRIB WALK

Where is the infant king of the Jews?
(Mt 2:2)

During the days between Christmas, New Year and back-to-school time, families are often looking for activities to engage in together, particularly ones that will take them out of the house. Perhaps families could use this time to take a crib walk. Design a plan for a short walk around the churches and chapels of the local area to visit the different cribs. It is an opportunity for a walk together and also to celebrate the real story of Christmas as a family. You might even designate an afternoon when parishioners are invited to meet together in the local town and share in the crib walk together.

Every parish designs its crib differently and this can be a creative way to encounter the Christmas story told through the crib in each parish church.

This activity obviously works more easily in towns and cities where there are several churches and chapels within walking distance of each other. Alternatively, you could suggest to families that, as they are out and about over the Christmas season, they look out for churches and stop by to visit the crib.

At each crib they might light a candle and say a prayer or even read the Christmas story together. At each crib a different member of the family can lead the prayer.

PRAYER AT THE CRIB

Lord Jesus
As I stand here before this crib
my thoughts turn to you, to Mary and to Joseph on
that first Christmas night.
It was there you welcomed the visit of the shepherds.
May I too receive visitors with a warm welcome and
an open heart.
You welcomed the Magi bringing their gifts of
Gold, frankincense and myrrh.
May these remind me of all that you have given for me.
Help me during the coming year to be more like you
each day.
Jesus, Mary and Joseph, pray for me. Amen.

The mystery of Christmas and the secret of Nazareth,
exude the beauty of family life!
(AL, 65)

14. HOLY FAMILY: BLESSING OF FAMILIES

Let the message of Christ,
in all its richness, find a home in you
(Col 3:16)

On the Sunday after Christmas Day the Church celebrates the feast of the Holy Family – a day when we too can celebrate with all the families in our parish communities.

Christmas Day is the day when we usually see the largest crowds in our churches so on this day give out an invitation to all families as they leave the church, or invite a parishioner to issue the invite verbally at the end of the Christmas Masses. Invite families to come the following Sunday to celebrate the feast of the Holy Family. During the celebration, each family will receive a special blessing.

At the end of Mass on the feast day of the Holy Family, invite families to come forward together to receive the blessing and give them a prayer card with the prayer for families to take home with them. If the crowd is very large or time is limited, the priest could give one blessing for all the families and then distribute the prayer cards as families leave the church.

PRAYER FOR FAMILIES

Jesus Christ, the Son of God,
left his heavenly home
to be born into a human family.
He was conceived by the power of the Holy Spirit,
born of the Virgin Mary,
and watched over by Joseph of Nazareth.
Today we ask God to bless all families gathered here
and make each of us more like Christ our Saviour.
Amen.

For individual blessings, invite each family to come forward
and to be blessed together with these words:

As you seek to live as family in the image of Jesus, Mary
and Joseph, the Holy Family, may God bless each of you
and those you love, in the name of the Father, the Son
and of the Holy Spirit. Amen.

*Every family should look to the icon
of the Holy family of Nazareth
(AL, 30)*

15. EPIPHANY: THE JOURNEY OF THE MAGI

We saw his star as it rose and have come to do him homage
(Mt 2:2)

This is an activity families, and indeed all parishioners, can partake in at home between Christmas Day and Feast of the Epiphany.

On the night of 25 December take the crib figures of the Magi and place them somewhere in your home, away from the crib. This marks the beginning of the journey of the Magi. Read together the story of the Magi. And so the journey begins.

Each night before bedtime move the Magi a little further along the way to Bethlehem. It is okay for them to take wrong turns – perhaps their journey was not straight forward! Then sit down together and talk about how the Magi are seeking Jesus and share with one another where you each met Jesus today on your journey.

The short conversation before bedtime will probably work best with the smaller children. Families with teenagers or adults/couples living together can decide when to have their conversation. It may work better at a meal time or another time of the day. Those living alone can take a moment to contemplate each day where Jesus was found on their journey that day.

After the conversation or time of contemplation, pray this family prayer:

FAMILY DAILY PRAYER

Dear God,

Thank you for the special journey you are about to take us on as a family.

Thank you for coming to this earth so we might each come to know you better

and see you at work in our lives each day.

Open our eyes to see you each day, as we open our hands and hearts to you

and what you want to teach us.

We love you, Jesus. Amen.

This journey of the figures of the Magi can be replicated in your parish church and begin each daily Mass with a pause to remember how Jesus revealed himself each day in the lives of those present. Then pray the prayer together.

Like the Magi, our families are invited to contemplate the Child and his Mother, to bow down and worship him
(AL, 30)

16. EPIPHANY: CELEBRATING ALL NATIONS

When they saw where the star had stopped, they were
overwhelmed with joy.
On entering the house, they saw the child with Mary his
mother; and they knelt down and paid him homage.
Then opening their treasure chests, they offered him gifts
of gold, frankincense, and myrrh
(Mt 2:10–11)

For your first parish Mass of the feast of the Epiphany, invite three families of different nationalities to each bring one of the figures of the Magi to the crib as part of the opening procession. Include all the members of each family in the procession even though each family will only bring one of the figures to the crib. Together we celebrate Christ coming as saviour of all people of the world.

This is a good way to open up our churches to include all who come to gather for worship, especially those who have come from overseas and chosen to make our parish their home.

The Church ... is the house of the Father,
where there is a place for everyone
(AL, 310)

LENT,
HOLY WEEK
AND
EASTER

17. ASH WEDNESDAY

See, I have set before you today, life and prosperity,
death and adversity
(Deut 30:15)

On Ash Wednesday many people come to Mass to receive the blessed ashes on their foreheads to mark the beginning of the season of Lent and as a reminder that we are called by God to remember from where we came and to what we shall return at the end of our earthly life. We are called each year to think about how we live our lives in relationship with God, with one another and with all of creation.

Today perhaps consider inviting families to become ministers to others by taking the blessed ashes to local schools and nursing homes in your parish.

At the end of your parish Mass invite those to be commissioned as ministers to come forward. This could be parents and grandparents taking ashes to the local primary school, young people taking ashes to their school or a family group taking ashes to the local nursing home. Be creative in who you invite to take on this ministry.

Give them the prepared service outlined below and the bowl of blessed ashes to take with them.

SERVICE OF ASHES FOR SCHOOLS AND NURSING HOMES IN YOUR PARISH

The bowls of blessed ashes to be brought from the church are placed in a prepared sacred space on a table near the altar.

GREETING

LEADER: On this first day of Lent, as we begin our journey, let us stand and mark ourselves with the sign of our faith: In the name of the Father, and of the Son and of the Holy Spirit.

OPENING PRAYER

LEADER:

> Father,
> Through our observance of Lent
> help us to understand the meaning
> of your Son's death and Resurrection,
> and teach us to reflect it in our lives.
> We ask this through Christ our Lord.
> Amen.

LEADER: Please be seated as we listen to the word of God.

A reading from the letter of St Paul to the Corinthians

So we are ambassadors for Christ, God making his appeal through us. We beseech you on behalf of Christ, be reconciled to God. For our sake he made him to be sin who knew no sin, so that in him we might become the righteousness of God.

Working together with him, then, we entreat you not to accept the grace of God in vain. For he says, 'At the acceptable time I have listened to you, and helped you on the day of salvation'. Behold, now is the acceptable time; behold, now is the day of salvation.

The Word of the Lord.

An appropriate psalm may be sung here.

A reading from the Holy Gospel according to Matthew

Beware of practising your piety before others in order to be seen by them; for then you will have no reward from your Father who is in heaven.

Thus, when you give alms, sound no trumpet before you, as the hypocrites do in the synagogues and in the streets, that they may be praised by others. Truly, I say to you, they have their reward. But when you give alms, do not let your left hand know what your right hand is doing, so that your alms may be in secret; and your Father who sees in secret will reward you.

And when you pray, you must not be like the hypocrites; for they love to stand and pray in the synagogues and at the street corners, that they may be seen by others. Truly, I say to you, they have their reward. But when you pray, go into your room and shut the door and pray to your Father who is in secret; and your Father who sees in secret will reward you.

And when you fast, do not look dismal, like the hypocrites, for they disfigure their faces that their fasting may be seen by others. Truly, I say to you, they have their reward. But when you fast, anoint your head and wash your face, that your fasting may not be seen by others but by your Father who is in secret; and your Father who sees in secret will reward you.

The Gospel of the Lord.

INVITATION TO A MOMENT OF SILENCE

LEADER: Let us reflect on these words in a moment of silence, as we prepare ourselves to receive the sign of our lenten journey.

DISTRIBUTION OF ASHES

LEADER: Will those who are to distribute the blessed ashes please come forward.

Either of the following accompany the signing of the cross with ashes on the forehead.

Remember you are dust and unto dust you shall return.
or
Turn away from sin and be faithful to the Gospel.

Ministers come forward, take ashes to their designated station (if in school setting) or receive ashes and begin distribution (if in nursing home).

Appropriate music may be played at this stage.

After distribution is complete, the ministers of the ashes wash their hands and return to their places.

OUR FATHER

LEADER: In Christ we are one. Together we stand and pray the prayer that he gave us.

Our Father who art in heaven ...

CLOSING PRAYER

LEADER:

Loving God,
as we make our lenten journey back to you
remain with us and guide us in the days ahead.
Help us to recognise and accept your constant care for
us
as we seek to deepen our faith and receive your mercy.
We make this our prayer through Christ our Lord.
Amen.

DISMISSAL

LEADER: And may God bless us and keep us as we leave this place and continue our journey of Lent. In the name of the Father, and of the Son and of the Holy Spirit.

ALL: Amen.

*This exhortation ... seeks to encourage everyone
to be a sign of mercy
(AL, 5)*

18. LENTEN FAMILY PRAYER SPACE

In the morning, long before dawn, he got up and left the house and went off to a lonely place and prayed there
(Mk 1:35)

As the daily routine of a family becomes busier and they spend less time together it is good to take stock of what is important, of what is most valuable. The season of Lent offers a space and a time to return our focus to our priorities. It can also help us to set new routines in our daily life as a family. Prayer is at the heart of family life. As the old saying goes, 'the family that prays together, stays together'. Perhaps there is a lesson in this for all of us!

At the beginning of Lent encourage every household in your parish to create a lenten prayer space, a visual daily reminder of the need to pause and to pray each day, giving thanks to God for blessings received, to pray for the needs of family, friends and our world, to pause and listen to the voice of God speaking to us each day.

The prayer space is also a significant reminder to visitors that this is a family that prays alone and together.

WHAT TO INCLUDE IN YOUR PRAYER SPACE FOR LENT
Begin with a purple cloth – the colour of penance

Add a crucifix – a reminder of Christ's death on the cross for us

Add some holy water – a reminder to us to bless ourselves as we begin each new day

A candle – this can be lit as the family comes together to pray

A bowl of sand – a reminder of Jesus' forty days in the desert

On Ash Wednesday bring home some of the blessed ashes from the Church – a reminder of our mortality

On St Patrick's Day add some shamrock – a reminder of God, Father, Son and Holy Spirit

On Mother's Day add a card of gratitude for your mother and a statue/picture of Our Blessed Lady

On Palm Sunday add the blessed palm branch you receive

On Easter Sunday change the colour of the cloth to white to symbolise Resurrection, bring home some of the newly blessed Easter water and add a vase of spring flowers from your garden

DAILY LENTEN PRAYER

Today Lord, I choose life,
I choose your love and the challenge to live it and share it,
I choose hope, even in moments of darkness,
I choose faith, accepting you as Lord and God,
I choose to let go of some part of my burdens,
Day by day, handing them over to you.
I choose to take hold of your strength and power
Ever more deeply in my life.
May this truly be for me a time of new life, of change,
challenge and growth.
May I come to Easter with a heart open to dying with you
And rising to new life, day by day.
Amen.

A few minutes can be found each day to come together
before the living God,
to tell him our worries, to ask for the needs of our family,
to pray for someone experiencing difficulty,
to ask for help in showing love,
to give thanks for life and for its blessings,
and to ask Our Lady to protect us ... this moment of prayer
can do immense good for our families
(AL, 318)

19. LENTEN BLESSINGS BOX

Always be joyful; pray constantly;
and for all things give thanks;
this is the will of God for you in Christ Jesus
(1 Th 5:18)

Before Lent begins find a box (a shoebox will work well for this activity) and sit down with children and grandchildren to decorate the box. Make a label saying 'Lenten Blessings' and attach it to the box.

Place the blessings box in a prominent place in your home. Prepare some small strips of paper and leave them next to the box. Each day during Lent, family members are invited to write one blessing they have received that day and place it into the blessings box.

You may have been blessed by:

- someone doing something kind for you
- someone praising you for work done well
- a smile received from a stranger
- a generous gift received
- the joy of sunshine, of raindrops, of spring flowers
- the blessing of new life

There is so much to be thankful for each day so the box should be easy to fill during the season of Lent.

Each Sunday of Lent open the box and sit together as a family to read out all the blessings you have received during the week.

Afterwords, say a prayer of thanksgiving together, then wrap the blessings from the week together and label them according to the Sunday. On Easter Sunday, take all the blessings from the box and celebrate together all your family has received over the season of Lent.

Three weeks before Lent begins, the parish can invite families to join in with this activity. Ask them to bring their home-made lenten blessings boxes to Mass on the First Sunday of Lent and bless the boxes and their owners.

Or invite families to bring their blessings boxes to Mass on Easter Sunday. Put them in a special place and give thanks prayerfully together for all the blessings of Lent received by families in the parish.

PRAYER OF THANKSGIVING FOR THE BLESSINGS RECEIVED

Each household can choose when to say this prayer – perhaps at the end of each day or at the end of each week.

Heavenly Father,
We thank you this day for all the blessings we have received from your goodness,
Those we have noticed, named and placed in our lenten blessings box and those that have gone unnoticed by us.
We pray for each other that we will continue through this season of Lent to stop, to notice and to give thanks for all that we receive from you each day.
This we ask through your Son, Jesus Christ in union with the Holy Spirit for ever and ever. Amen.

The spirituality of family love
is made up of thousands of small but real gestures
(AL, 315)

20. FAST – PRAY – GIVE

*Then Jesus was led by the Spirit out into the desert to be
put to the test by the devil.
He fasted for forty days and forty nights
(Mt 4:1)*

The season of Lent is marked by three actions:

FASTING: Giving up something that we enjoy, often our favourite food, and giving the cost of those items to the poor.

PRAYING: Taking more time each day to pray. Prayer is our conversation with God. It requires us to pause in our daily routine and make time not just to ask God for things we desire but also to listen to the voice of God in our minds and in our hearts.

GIVING: Sharing from all that we have with those who are in need. This requires us to make sacrifices, be they large or small, and to give to those who are in need. This can be a monetary sacrifice, giving away items we have been keeping but do not need or giving our time to assist others who require our support and our help.

For Lent, invite families to make several cards, each one bearing one of the three actions, fast: pray, give. Every morning of Lent each member of the family should take one card and engage in that action during the day. At the end of the day the cards are put back ready for the next day. If they wish, families can share with each other at the end of the day what they did to engage in their action as they went about their routine.

Alternatively, one card could be chosen each day and all the members of the family could undertake the same lenten action.

Creative families might also choose to make cube/dice that can be thrown by each member of the family in the morning to decide what Lenten action each one will undertake that day. There are six faces on a cube so each action will get two faces.

If the family is centred on Christ,
he will unify and illumine its entire life
(AL, 317)

21. THE CROSS OF HOPE

May he enlighten the eyes of your mind
so that you can see what hope his call holds for you
(Eph 1:18)

Most of our parish churches place a large wooden cross in the sanctuary space during the lenten season. If you don't already do this, perhaps make arrangements for it this year. It is just a bare, plain wooden cross, sized to fit your sanctuary space or other chosen space in your church where people have easy access to it.

Next to the cross place a basket with cards and a few pens/ pencils and some Blu Tack as required for this activity. Over the season of Lent invite parishioners to come quietly and in their own time take a card on which they write their message of hope. What are they hoping for this lenten season? It may be for themselves, a family member, the local community, a friend or neighbour, the Church or the world. They then attach their hope to the cross. Each day during Lent prepare one of your Prayers of the Faithful at daily Mass to reflect the hopes placed on the cross.

On Holy Saturday night you can offer all these hopes of the lenten season to the Lord in your Easter prayer.

All family life is a 'shepherding' in mercy. Each of us, by our
love and care, leaves a mark on the life of others
(AL, 322)

22. FAMILY STATIONS OF THE CROSS

In truth this man was the Son of God
(Mk 15:39)

During Lent, and especially on Good Friday, many people gather in our parishes to pray the Stations of the Cross. This year consider inviting fourteen different families to lead your parishioners in this prayer. Distribute the stations among these families and let it become a moment of family catechesis as parents, children and grandparents talk together about the scene at their station and prepare to lead the prayer for the parish at that particular station.

On the day, seat each family near their station and as the procession approaches, the family should stand and lead the reflection and prayer together. This might mean less uniformity to the prayer but there can be great unity in the diversity of prayer as each family shares part of the story of the Way of the Cross.

In practice you will probably need to provide an outline structure so there is some familiarity to allow the congregation to participate in the responses.

When inviting families, try to create a balance. Include families with small children, teenagers, adult children at home, then also consider single people, couples with no children and elderly people. Let this prayer together be as inclusive of the different families that make up your parish community as possible. You will need fourteen families so this offers an opportunity to include a cross section of parishioners.

Enabling families to take up their role as active agents of the family apostolate calls for an effort at evangelisation and catechesis inside the family

(AL, 200)

23. HOLY THURSDAY: NEWLY BLESSED OILS

Acclaim the Lord all the earth,
serve the Lord with gladness,
come into his presence with songs of joy!
(Ps 100:1–2)

During Holy Week, usually on the morning of Holy Thursday, the bishops and priests of the diocese gather in the cathedral for what is known as the Chrism Mass when the new oils that will be used in administering the sacraments across the whole diocese are consecrated or blessed by the bishop. During the Eucharistic Prayer the bishop consecrates the oil of chrism, while later in the Mass he will bless the oil of catechumens and the oil of the sick. These oils are then distributed to all the parishes and churches in the diocese.

At the evening Mass of the Lord's Supper it is fitting to bring the newly consecrated and blessed oils into the church in the opening procession. When the procession comes to the sanctuary, those carrying the oils stand to one side. Then, before the celebrant begins the Mass, invite one of the parish ministers of the word to read the commentary as the oils are presented.

Consider inviting the following parishioners to bring the oils in the procession:

Oil of catechumens: A family preparing for the Baptism of their child

Oil of the sick: A family who care for someone who is sick

Oil of chrism: A family preparing a child for confirmation or a family preparing for the ordination of a son

Put the emphasis on the family bringing the oil in procession and presenting it at the opening of the Mass rather than on just one person.

MASS OF THE LORD'S SUPPER
Suggested text as the oils are presented.

The Chrism Mass for the diocese was celebrated in the cathedral this morning. The holy oils to be used in the sacraments during the year in all parishes of the diocese were blessed at this Mass.

The oil of catechumens is presented by ....
whose son/daughter will be baptised here in our parish on

....
It will be used to anoint all who are to be baptised during the coming year.

The oil of the sick is presented by ....
who care for .... in their home.
It will be used to anoint each person who receives the Sacrament of the Sick in our parish during the coming year.

The holy chrism is presented by ....
whose son will be ordained to the priesthood in our parish/ diocese this year.

or

The holy chrism is presented by ....
whose son/daughter .... received/
will receive the Sacrament of Confirmation here in our parish
on ....

All the children and adults who are baptised and confirmed
in our parish during the year will be anointed with chrism.
Priests are also anointed with chrism at ordination.

We welcome the blessings which the Lord sends us
through the ministry of the Church.

Faith is God's gift, received in Baptism, and not our own
work, yet parents are the means that
God uses for it to grow and develop
(AL, 287)

24. EASTER SUNDAY: EASTER EGG HUNT

They have taken the Lord out of the tomb, she said,
and we don't know where they have put him
(Jn 20:2)

This idea is aimed especially at the younger members of the parish community but also offers an opportunity to get teenagers involved in hiding the Easter eggs in the church grounds.

All you need is lots of small Easter eggs and volunteers to hide them. Make some easy to find so that the very small children have a chance to find some too! Keep a few for any child who doesn't find an egg – let no child be disappointed.

At the end of Easter Sunday Mass, invite the children to gather together. Have someone tell them the story of the Easter egg, reminding them of the stone that was rolled away revealing the empty tomb from which Jesus had risen. Explain that this is what we celebrate today.

The Story of the Easter Egg
Today we are celebrating the Resurrection of Jesus and most of you will have already received an Easter egg made from your favourite chocolate. But do you know why you have been given an egg?

Eggs are the symbol of new life, of new birth. So the egg you receive today reminds you of the new life of Jesus as he rose from the tomb where his body had been placed on Good Friday when it was taken down from the cross. When his body had been buried in the tomb by his friends a very large stone was placed across the entrance to prevent anyone from entering. The Easter egg also represents this stone – as it was rolled away and let Jesus rise again from the tomb.

So as you go now and hunt for the Easter eggs – remember the stone that was rolled away and remember Jesus who rose from the dead for us that we might have new life.

After the story is read, invite the children to go out into the garden to hunt for the Easter eggs. If your parish has no garden or grounds the Easter eggs can be hidden around an area of the church.

If you have only a small number of children attending your parish why not ask them to give out Easter eggs to everyone as they leave Mass.

Children are a wonderful gift from God ... through them the
Lord renews the world
(AL, 222)

FEAST DAYS

25. BAPTISM OF THE LORD: CELEBRATING THE NEWLY BAPTISED

Let the little children come to me, and do not stop them;
for it is to such as these that the kingdom of heaven belongs
(Mt 19:14)

On the Sunday after the Feast of the Epiphany we celebrate the Baptism of the Lord by John the Baptist in the River Jordan. This feast is a timely reminder to us all of our own Baptism and the promises made by our parents and godparents on our behalf.

Choose one of your Sunday Masses and invite all the families, parents, grandparents and godparents to attend with the children who were baptised in the past year. In the opening procession of the Mass invite a member of your parish Baptism preparation team to bring forward the names of all the children baptised during the year.

After the homily, invite all the parents and godparents to come forward into the sanctuary with the children who were baptised and offer a special blessing for them.

It is a reminder to the whole parish that every year we welcome new members into our faith community. And on this day the whole community celebrates and welcomes them into the family of the parish.

BLESSING OF THE CHILDREN BAPTISED DURING THE PAST YEAR

PRESIDER: Brothers and sisters, let us praise and thank the Lord, who took little children into his arms and blessed them. Praised be the Lord now and for ever.

ALL: Amen.

PRESIDER: When he came into the world, our Lord, the Son of God, became a child and grew in wisdom, age, and grace in the eyes of God and of all who knew him. Jesus welcomed children, believed in their dignity, and held them up as a model for all who are seeking the kingdom of God.

Children need the help and example of parents, grandparents, godparents, family members and indeed the whole Christian community if they are to develop their individual gifts, and their moral, mental, and physical powers, and so reach human and Christian maturity.

Let us therefore ask for God's blessing, so that we will devote ourselves to the Christian upbringing of these children and so that they will accept willingly the guidance they need.

The Lord Jesus held up to all his followers the simplicity and trust of children as a condition for entering the kingdom of heaven.

PRAYER OF BLESSING

Lord, our God, out of the speech of little children you have fashioned a hymn of praise. Look with kindness on these children whom the faith of the Church commends to your tender care. Your son, born of the Virgin Mary, gladly welcomed little children, so we too, in our parish community, show them that same welcome among us as brothers and sisters in him.

Jesus took the children in his arms, blessed them, and held them up as an example for all.

We pray that you, Father, will also send your blessing on these children, so that they may grow in Christian maturity and, by the power of the Holy Spirit, become Christ's witnesses in the world, spreading and defending the faith.

We ask this through Christ our Lord.

ALL: Amen.

The family is the setting in which a new life is not only born but also welcomed as a gift of God
(AL, 166)

26. SAINT BRIGID: MAKING AND BLESSING THE CROSS

If you have hope, this will make you cheerful
(Rm 12:13)

Saint Brigid is the patron of Ireland, along with St Patrick and St Colmcille, so it is good that her story and the traditions surrounding her are handed on from one generation to the next.

Invite parishioners to collect the reeds needed to make the St Brigid's cross and then invite them to meet to make the crosses together.

This is an all-ages activity! It is usually the older members of the congregation who teach the younger members how to make the crosses. As the crosses are woven tell the story of St Brigid, and have colouring pages for the very young members so they too can join in celebrating Brigid.

On the feast day, 1 February, bring the crosses to Mass for the blessing and encourage families to take them home and place them on the wall of their houses to ask Brigid's blessing for the coming year. Give each parishioner the prayer card with the prayer to say when hanging the cross on the wall of their home.

Story of St Brigid

Saint Brigid was born around 450 AD in Faughart, a few miles north of Dundalk in Co. Louth. Her father was a pagan chieftain called Dubhthach, who lived on a big farm. Her mother, Brocca, was a Christian slave who was baptised by St Patrick.

Brigid was a very generous, kind and caring person. When she was a teenager she helped to look after her father's house and she often gave away much of their food and clothes to people who needed them. Locally, Brigid was known for her generosity to the poor, and one story tells how as a child she once gave away her mother's entire store of butter. Knowing that this would get her into trouble, she prayed to God that the butter would be replenished and her prayers were heard.

Brigid ultimately decided to give her life to God as a nun, and with seven other young women she founded a convent in Kildare. She needed land to build her convent and church, so she went to the King of Leinster and asked for some land. The King said he would only give her the land that her cloak would cover. Brigid agreed. When she laid it down, Brigid's cloak grew and grew and spread over a few acres of land. Here, Brigid built her church and convent. The name Kildare means 'church of the oak'.

It is likely that the pagans worshipped here and Brigid wanted it to be a Christian place of worship. It is said that there was a fire in Kildare which was kept burning by the pagans to worship pagan gods. Brigid used this custom and the light of the fire came to be known and understood as the Light of Christ. The flame of Brigid or *Solas Bhride* still burns in Kildare today. By the time Brigid died around 525 AD, Kildare was a place of learning, prayer and worship. She certainly sowed the seeds of God's love there.

It is believed that Brigid travelled around Ireland in a chariot, healing people and restoring speech to those who could not talk. Perhaps the best known story is of her visit to a dying pagan chieftain (in some versions we are told that it was her own father). While she prayed, she took rushes from the floor and wove them into a cross. While she was weaving she told the chieftain all about Jesus and how he had died on the cross. The chieftain asked her many questions and was baptised and became a Christian before he died. Brigid's crosses are now made each St Brigid's Day.

People like to hang the crosses in their homes and sheds to protect themselves, their homes and their animals from harm.

TRADITIONAL IRISH PRAYERS FOR ST BRIGID'S DAY
BLESSING OF THE ST BRIGID'S CROSS

Father of all creation and Lord of Light,
you have given us life and entrusted your creation to us
to use it and to care for it.
We ask you to bless these crosses made of green rushes
in memory of holy Brigid,
who used the cross to recall and to teach your Son's life,
death and Resurrection.
May these crosses be a sign of our sharing in the paschal
mystery of your Son and a sign of your protection of
our lives, our land and its creatures through Brigid's
intercession during the coming year and always. We ask
this through Christ our Lord.

The crosses are sprinkled with holy water.

May the blessing of God, Father, Son and Holy Spirit, be
on these crosses and on the places where they hang and
on everyone who looks at them. Amen.

PRAYER AS THE CROSS IS PLACED ON THE WALL OF THE HOME

May Brigid bless the house wherein we dwell.
Bless every fireside, every wall and door.
Bless every heart that beats beneath its roof.
Bless every hand that toils to bring its joy.
Bless every foot that walks through.
May Brigid bless the house that shelters us.
Amen.

Moments of family prayer and acts of devotion can be more powerful than any catechism class or classroom
(AL, 288)

27. SAINT VALENTINE: CELEBRATING LOVE AND MARRIAGE

Love one another, as I have loved you
(Jn 15:12)

There are two ways offered here that can be used on this feast day, 14 February, or at the vigil. They can be merged together in the one celebration or offered separately as the parish chooses.

Celebrating engaged couples who are preparing for marriage
Invite engaged couples to come for a special blessing of the engagement ring and of their love and commitment to one another on this day.

PRAYER OF BLESSING

We know that all of us need God's blessing at all times; but at the time of their engagement to be married, Christians are in particular need of grace as they prepare themselves to form a new family.

Let us pray, then, for God's blessing to come upon this couple: that as they await the day of their wedding, they will grow in mutual respect and in their love for one another; that through their companionship and prayer together they will prepare themselves for marriage.

Lord God, the source of all love, the wise plan of your providence has brought these young people together. As

they prepare themselves for the sacrament of marriage and pray for your grace, grant that, strengthened by your blessing, they may grow in their respect for one another and cherish each other with a sincere love.
We ask this through Christ our Lord.
Amen.

CELEBRATING MARRIAGE

Invite couples from your parish, especially those celebrating significant anniversaries and those who were married in your parish the previous year. Let these couples have a special place in your celebration of Mass, inviting one couple to be ministers of the word, another to be ministers of the Eucharist and another to bring forward the offertory gifts.

The focus of the homily should be love and marriage. Afterwards invite the couples to come forward for a special marriage blessing.

PRAYER OF BLESSING

Almighty and eternal God, you have so exalted the unbreakable bond of marriage that it has become the sacramental sign of your son's union with the Church as his spouse.

Look with favour on these couples whom you have united in marriage, as they ask for your help and the protection of the Virgin Mary. They pray that in good times and in bad they will grow in love for each other; that they will resolve to be of one heart in the bond of peace.

Lord, in their struggles let them rejoice that you are near to help them; in their needs let them know that you are there to rescue them; in their joys let them see that you are the source and completion of every happiness.
We ask this through Christ our Lord.
Amen.

It is possible to bring these two celebrations together, having the two blessings separately but within the same eucharistic celebration.

Marriage is a gift from the Lord
(AL, 61)

28. SAINT PATRICK: PRAYING FOR EMIGRANTS

I have made you a light for the nations,
so that my salvation may reach the ends of the earth
(Acts 13:47)

Over recent years many families have said goodbye to their loved ones who have emigrated for work or to travel. This has rekindled the memories of past years when large numbers of people left Ireland to find work to enable them to send money home to their families. Hence, today the Irish diaspora stretches far and wide across the world – not forgetting the many thousands who took up the staff of Patrick to go as missionaries to far-flung lands. Today we remember all who left these shores for whatever reason.

Prepare name cards for the St Patrick's Day Masses on 17 March and as they arrive into the church invite parishioners to write the names of family members and friends who have left Ireland and celebrate St Patrick in other lands. Invite them to place the cards into a basket at the church door. The basket can then be brought forward by one family as part of the opening procession of the Mass and placed in front of the altar, making them the focus of prayer today.

PRAYER FOR EMIGRANTS

Bless all those who have left our country, for many
different reasons, and now live in other lands.
Give them a strong faith so that they will always put
their trust in you and make you known by the loving

example of their lives.

Console those who are lonely because they are separated from those they love.

Help all missionaries who are working far from home who followed your commission to make disciples of all nations and to make your love known to all peoples.

Bless our people overseas who are sick or in prison and in need of your comfort and strength.

Grant your eternal welcome to our emigrants who have died and are buried in other lands.

Amen.

We need to renew the covenant between the family and the Christian community

(AL, 279)

29. SAINT ANTHONY: BLESSING OF LILIES FOR THE SICK

Cure those ... who are sick and say,
the kingdom of God is very near to you
(Lk 10:9)

Lilies have special significance as we celebrate the feast of St Anthony and not just because they are in bloom around this time of year. The traditional image of St Anthony holding the lily comes from two important events relating to the saint.

On 13 June 1680, in the church at Mentosca d'Agesco in Austria, someone placed a lily in the hand of his statue. For an entire year the lily remained fragrant and fully alive without wilting. The following year it grew two more blooms, so that the church was filled with the fragrance of lilies.

A little over a century later, during the French Revolution, the Franciscans were forced to abandon their parishioners on the island of Corsica. The people refused to give up their devotions, although they had no choice in the matter of the sacraments because they had no priests. They invoked the intercession of St Anthony. On 13 June they erected a shrine to the saint in the deserted church; the shrine included lilies in his honour. Months later the blooms were still fresh as if they had just been placed there.

Permission to bless lilies in honour of the saint was given by Pope Leo XIII. Many favours have been granted through this devotion, such as help for the sick who have been touched by the petals of the blessed flowers. The Church holds that these blessed flowers are sacramentals.

It is because of this last tradition that on the feast day of St Anthony we are invited to bless lilies and take them to those who are sick, that they bring their fragrance and the reminder of St Anthony's prayers to them. Invite parishioners to bring lilies to Mass for blessing and then to go in twos to bring them to the homes of those who are sick in the parish community.

BLESSING OF THE LILIES

PRESIDER: Let us pray. God, the creator and preserver of the human race, the lover of holy purity, the giver of supernatural grace, and the dispenser of everlasting salvation; bless these lilies which we, your humble servants, present to you today as an act of thanksgiving and in honour of St Anthony, your confessor, and with a request for your blessing. Pour out on them, by the saving sign of the holy cross, your dew from on high. You in your great kindness have given them to man, and endowed them with a sweet fragrance to lighten the burden of the sick. Therefore, let them be filled with such power that, whether they are used by the sick, or kept in homes or other places, or devoutly carried on one's person, they may serve to drive out evil spirits, safeguard holy chastity, and turn away illness – all this through the prayers of St Anthony – and finally impart to your servants grace and peace; through Christ our Lord.

ALL: Amen.

The presider sprinkles the lilies with holy water.

PRESIDER: Let us pray. We beg you, O Lord, that your people may be helped by the constant and devout intercession of Blessed Anthony, your illustrious confessor. May he assist us to be worthy of your grace in this life, and to attain everlasting joys in the life to come; through Christ our Lord.

ALL: Amen.

The lilies are distributed to the people.

Care and concern for the final stages of life are all the more necessary today ... many families show us that it is possible to approach the last stages of life by emphasising the importance of a person's sense of fulfilment and participation in the Lord's paschal mystery
(AL, 48)

30. PENTECOST: CELEBRATING ALL NATIONS

The spirit of the Lord has filled the whole world
(Wis 1:7)

Pentecost Sunday is a day when we celebrate the coming of the Holy Spirit upon the Apostles, empowering them to go forth and take the Good News of Jesus Christ to all the peoples.

Today we celebrate all who have come to live among us, making our parishes their home. This feast lends itself to celebrating the diversity of people who make up our parish communities so we can bring this to our liturgy.

Display the flags of the different countries represented in your parish in the church and/or include the colours in your floral displays. Better still, invite different families to create displays about their country around the church.

After the second reading of our Mass is the Sequence for Pentecost. Invite parishioners from different countries to lead this prayer, taking a verse each and reading it in their native tongue. Invite them to wear their national dress for this participation.

SEQUENCE FOR PENTECOST

Prayed after the second reading and before the Gospel Acclamation

Holy Spirit, Lord of light,
From thy clear celestial height
Thy pure beaming radiance give.

Come thou Father of the poor,
Come with treasures which endure;
Come, thou light of all that live!

Thou of all consolers best,
Thou, the soul's delightful guest,
Dost refreshing peace bestow;

Thou in toil art comfort sweet;
Pleasant coolness in the heat;
Solace in the midst of woe.

Light immortal, light divine,
Visit thou these hearts of thine,
And our inmost being fill:

If thou take thy grace away,
Nothing pure in man will stay;
All his good is turned to ill.

Heal our wounds, our strength renew;
On our dryness pour thy dew;
Wash the stains of guilt away:

Bend the stubborn heart and will;
Melt the frozen, warm the chill;
Guide the steps that go astray.

Thou on us who evermore
Thee confess and thee adore,
With thy sevenfold gifts descend:

Give us comfort when we die;
Give us life with thee on high;
Give us joys that never end.

As the Our Father is introduced, invite those present to pray in their native language, so creating a cacophony of prayer to the father of all peoples.

After Mass, celebrate together with traditional music, story, song and food from the many nationalities that make up your parish community.

Human mobility ... can prove to be a genuine enrichment
for both families that migrate and countries
that welcome them
(AL, 46)

31. SAINTS JOACHIM AND ANNE: CELEBRATING GRANDPARENTS

Let us praise ... our ancestors
(Eccl 44:1)

On 26 July, we celebrate Joachim and Anne, the parents of Mary and grandparents of Jesus. In the weeks beforehand, ask the children to invite their grandparents to come to Mass with them for this feast day, or the grandparents to invite their grandchildren.

Invite several grandparents and their grandchildren to participate in the Mass through readings, Prayers of the Faithful, offertory procession, etc.

At the end of the Mass, before the blessing, invite the grandparents and their grandchildren to come forward and pray this prayer written by Pope Benedict for grandparents.

PRAYER FOR GRANDPARENTS

Lord Jesus,
you were born of the Virgin Mary,
the daughter of Saints Joachim and Anne.
Look with love on grandparents the world over.
Protect them! They are a source of enrichment
for families, for the Church and for all of society.
Support them! As they grow older,
may they continue to be for their families
strong pillars of Gospel faith,
guardians of noble domestic ideals,
living treasuries of sound religious traditions.

Make them teachers of wisdom and courage,
that they may pass on to future generations the fruits
of their mature human and spiritual experience.
Lord Jesus,
help families and society
to value the presence and roles of grandparents.
May they never be ignored or excluded,
but always encounter respect and love.
Help them to live serenely and to feel welcomed
in all the years of life which you give them.
Mary, Mother of all the living,
keep grandparents constantly in your care,
accompany them on their earthly pilgrimage,
and by your prayers, grant that all families
may one day be reunited in our heavenly homeland,
where you await all humanity
for the great embrace of life without end.
Amen.

*Very often it is grandparents who ensure that the most
important values are passed down to their grandchildren*
(AL, 192)

32. SAINT FRANCIS: BLESSING OF PETS AND ANIMALS

God said, let the earth produce every kind of living creature
(Gn 1:24)

Saint Francis was known for his care and love of all creation so his feast day, 4 October, is an opportunity to invite parishioners, in particular families and children, to bring their pets to the church grounds for a special blessing and prayer service. In rural communities it is an opportunity to invite local farmers to bring along small farm animals to participate in the gathering.

Working animals in your parish community could also be included; for example, guide dogs, assistance dogs, dogs or horses of the Gardaí/police service, military horses.

You may need to set some limits for safety reasons, such as: children bringing pets must be accompanied by a parent/guardian; all dogs or larger animals must be kept on leads or reins. Ensure that you have a parishioner who has knowledge of animals on hand to assist.

PRAYER AND BLESSING OF THE ANIMALS

O God, you have done all things wisely; in your goodness you have made us in your image and given us care over other living things.

Reach out with your gentle hand and grant that these animals we bring with us today serve our needs, as pets and companions, to assist us and to keep us safe. We ask that your bounty in the resources of this life may move us to seek more confidently the goal of eternal life through Christ our Lord. Amen.

The animals and their owners are now sprinkled with holy water. All make the Sign of the Cross.

May God, who created the animals of this earth as a help to us, continue to protect and sustain us with the grace his blessing brings, now and for ever. Amen.

Conclude by singing together a suitable hymn, such as, 'Praise God from Whom all Blessings Flow', 'All Things Bright and Beautiful', 'For the Beauty of the Earth'.

In the family we learn closeness, care and respect
for others
(AL, 276)

THROUGH THE YEAR

33. MOTHER'S DAY AND FATHER'S DAY

He went down with them ... to Nazareth and lived
under their authority
(Lk 2:1–52)

These two days offer us an opportunity to give thanks in our liturgies for the vocation of parents and their role in giving life to children and handing on the faith to them.

On Mother's Day (Laetare Sunday, Fourth Sunday of Lent) and Father's Day (Third Sunday of June) ask children of all ages to invite their mother or father to join with them for Mass. During the Mass offer prayers of thanksgiving for mothers or fathers, remembering especially those who have died and now live with God in heaven.

At the end of Mass, before the final blessing, invite mothers or fathers (depending on which day you are celebrating) to come forward or to stand for a special prayer and blessing of thanksgiving.

PRAYERS FOR MOTHERS

O loving Lord, we thank you, for the gift of motherhood.
You have created mothers in love and blessed them
with children. May they be granted the gifts of courage,
perseverance and good health to face each new day with
faith and hope in your abiding love. May all families find
in the strength of your love the priceless gift of peace
and so bear witness to your glory.
Amen.

As Mary was the model of prayer, of love, and of
obedience to the will of God, by your grace make
mothers holy and rich with your gifts.
Bind families together in the bonds of peace and safety
so that mothers will feel nurtured by love.
May all mothers enjoy good health and spiritual
well-being to enable them to care for their families.
We commend to your loving care all mothers who have
gone before us and now share in your heavenly home
with Mary and all the saints.
This we ask through Christ our Lord.
Amen.

Mothers are always ... witnesses to tenderness,
dedication and moral strength
(AL, 174)

PRAYER FOR FATHERS

God our Father,
you govern and protect your people
and shepherd them with a father's love.
You place a father in a family
as a sign of your love, care, and constant protection.
May fathers everywhere be faithful
to the example shown in the scriptures:
steadfast in love, forgiving transgressions, sustaining
the family,
caring for those in need.
Give your wisdom to fathers
that they may encourage and guide their children.

Keep them healthy so they may support their family.
Guide every father
with the spirit of your love
that they may grow in holiness
and draw their family ever closer to you.
We remember today especially all fathers you have taken
home to yourself.
May they enjoy eternal peace with you.
Amen.

*A father ... helps the child to perceive the limits of life, to be
open to the challenges of the wider world
(AL, 175)*

*The union between the Lord and his faithful ones is
expressed in terms of parental love
(AL, 28)*

34. NOVEMBER, WE REMEMBER

Hope in him, hold firm, take heart.
Hope in the Lord!
(Ps 26:14)

During the month of November we remember especially all our loved ones who have died. The Church calendar gives us two days, the feast All Saints (1 November) followed by the Commemoration of all the Faithful Departed (2 November).

During this month your parish may host a special Mass of remembrance when you invite families who have been bereaved during the past year to come and remember their departed loved one. Send out special invitations to the families of all who have died during the year to come and join you in remembering. On the day have candles prepared and invite the families to bring forward the candle to the sanctuary to place in memory of their loved one. At the end of the Mass you can give them the candle to take home.

It is an opportunity to remind families of their departed loved ones, encouraging parents and grandparents to share the stories of the generations who have gone before them. As you invite parishioners to prepare their list of departed loved ones for the altar book of the dead, encourage this as a family activity and an opportunity to share the stories of their ancestors.

In November, many parishes also have their blessing of graves. This year, instead of the priest preforming the blessing, bless the water and invite families to come and use it to bless their own family graves. Ask them, too, to notice if there is a grave near them with no one to bless it. Invite them to spend a few moments in quiet prayer there too, remembering the holy souls who have no one present to pray for and bless them.

If your parish holds its blessing of graves in the summer months, you can adapt this activity to use then rather than in November.

Those who love are capable of speaking words of comfort, strength, consolation and encouragement
(AL, 100)

At times family life is challenged by the death of a loved one. We cannot fail to offer the light of faith as a support to families
(AL, 253)

35. SEND A CARD

I shall not forget you.
Look, I have engraved you on the palms of my hands
(Is 49:15–16)

Throughout the year in our parishes there are many celebrations in which the sacraments of the Church are administered; however, the parish community is not usually present to share in the joy of these occasions. Why not ask your parish pastoral council to be responsible for sending cards to mark these occasions on behalf of the parish community, including prayerful greetings and good wishes to:

- couples who get married in your church
- people from your parish who get married elsewhere
- parents who bring a child to be baptised
- children who make their first Holy Communion
- those who receive the Sacrament of Confirmation
- adults who receive the sacraments having participated in the RCIA process

Sending a card is a small gesture to show that the parish community is praying for them and thinking of them as they celebrate these significant milestones in their lives.

If you are a parish that has shared in the joy of an ordination to priesthood or the profession into religious life of a parishioner, send them a card on the anniversary each year to let them know that the parish continues to remember them and pray for them.

Each of us, by our love and care,
leaves a mark on the lives of others
(AL, 322)

36. PREPARING FOR BAPTISM

The parents of Jesus took him ... to present him to the Lord
(Lk 2:22)

When parents approach the parish seeking the sacrament of Baptism for their child, the parish is offered an opportunity to engage with them in a significant and meaningful way.

It is important that we do not just set the date, complete the form, and wait for the family to turn up at the church at the scheduled time. Parish communities need to train parishioners to meet with parents to prepare for the sacrament. They are celebrating a new chapter in the life of their family, whether it is their first child or an addition to their family. As this new chapter opens, it is important that the Church is involved. When trained parishioners meet with the parents the parish is engaging in some aspect of faith formation so that Baptism becomes more than just a day out for family and friends and leads rather to an opening of hearts and minds to regular participation in the life of the faith community that is welcoming this child.

By organising and running this sacramental preparation, a parish not only baptises and welcomes a child into the faith community but also gives parents a greater understanding of the responsibility they are taking on to raise their child in the practice of the faith.

By meeting with parents, the members of the parish Baptism preparation team become the human face of the parish community, there to welcome the parents and their child into the Christian community; thereby living the phrase from the introduction to the baptismal rite, 'The Christian community welcomes you with great joy'.

Training for parishioners to undertake this ministry will need to include a full understanding of the rite of Baptism in its movement, symbols, anointing, gestures and blessings. Alongside this, an understanding of how to journey with parents to help them to understand the commitment they are making by requesting Baptism for their child. The training will include theory and practice as well as the practical aspects of how best to approach this preparation with parents; for example, through home visits or group sessions? This will probably depend on the size of the parish and the average number of Baptisms celebrated. Many dioceses will already have this training available for parishes.

The Church assumes a valuable role in supporting families,
starting with Christian initiation,
through welcoming communities
(AL, 84)

With their prayers, parents prepare for Baptism,
entrusting their baby to Jesus
(AL, 169)

37. CELEBRATING WITH THOSE CONFIRMED

They were all filled with the Holy Spirit
(Acts 2:4)

Pentecost Sunday offers an opportunity for the parish to invite those children who received the Sacrament of Confirmation this year to come to Mass with their parents and sponsors to celebrate with the parish community.

Let those who were confirmed walk in as part of the opening procession of the Mass and address them directly in the homily. Before the closing blessing of the Mass, invite two parishioners to lead the following prayer for the children. This is something the members of the parish pastoral council could lead as part of their ministry in the parish. After the prayer give each child a certificate to mark their Confirmation.

PRAYER FOR THOSE CONFIRMED IN OUR PARISH THIS YEAR

READER 1: Today we have gathered to celebrate the coming of the Holy Spirit onto the Apostles in the Upper Room and to offer our support and encouragement to the children of our parish schools who received the Sacrament of Confirmation this year. And so we invite the children to gather here in front of the altar as we pray for them.

READER 2: On the day of your Confirmation you received the gifts of the Holy Spirit, now we pray that in your life you may experience the fruits of those seven gifts each day.

READER 1: We pray that you may live in peace and harmony with all your family and friends.

READER 2: We pray that you may wait patiently for God's plan to unfold in your life.

READER 1: We pray that you may walk this earth gently, showing respect for all of God's creation.

READER 2: We pray that you will act with self-control in all you do in your life.

READER 1: We pray that you will show kindness to all who need your care.

READER 2: We pray that you will be faithful witnesses to the Gospel message of Jesus throughout your life.

READER 1: We pray that you may see the goodness in all that you meet.

READER 2: We pray that your life will be filled with joy and happiness.

READER 1: We pray that you may give and receive love each day of your life.

READER 2: Today, as a parish community, we offer you our continued prayers as you move forward in your lives witnessing to the gift of the Holy Spirit among us.

READER 1: To mark this special year for you we give you these certificates as a remembrance of your Confirmation.

Other members of the parish (parish pastoral council) come forward to distribute the certificates.

Through the Church, marriage and the family receive
the grace of the Holy Spirit from Christ,
in order to bear witness to God's love
(AL, 71)

38. PRAYING FOR THOSE SITTING EXAMS

I am quite confident that the One who began a good work
in you will go on completing it
(Phil 1:6)

Every year in May and June young people from our parishes sit exams in university, college and school. These can be anxious days for them and for their parents. The parish community can become the hub of prayer during these times.

Create a space in your church and invite young people, their parents, grandparents and other parishioners to write the names of those sitting exams on a board or on cards. Place these in a basket in the prayer space and invite parishioners to pray each day for those who have been named. In this space you can place a candle and other symbols to remind the parishioners of the young people at this time.

You can also encourage the sick and housebound of the parish to join in with this prayer intention in May and June by publishing the prayer in the parish newsletter or taking a prayer card to them when you visit.

PRAYER FOR THOSE SITTING EXAMS

Lord, pour out your Spirit of Wisdom on these students:
help them to remain calm,
to attend carefully to the questions asked,
to think clearly, to remember accurately,
and to express themselves well.
Grant that they may reflect on the best of the work

they have done and the best of the teaching they have
received.
Accept their best efforts in these examinations
and in the great test of life on earth.
May your love be upon them, O Lord,
as they place all their trust in you.
We ask this through Christ our Lord.
Amen.

[Parents] in educating [children] … build up the Church
(AL, 85)

39. ICE-CREAM SUNDAY

And who is my neighbour?
(Lk 10:29)

Many families in our communities are blessed with special children who need extra care and attention throughout their lives. Parents and siblings of these children speak of the joy they bring to their lives each day. In our society many charities and support groups assist these families in their caring role and most rely on donations.

One such charity, Down Syndrome Ireland, invites us each year during May and June to host ice-cream parties to raise funds to assist them in carrying out their work. In our parishes we can be part of this fun activity by hosting an ice-cream Sunday. Offer ice-cream to all parishioners after Mass one weekend and collect donations. This initiative is sponsored by an ice-cream company and so all you need to host a party is provided you when you register on www. downsyndrome.ie.

Some parishes have successfully combined this activity with the feast of Corpus Christi, inviting families to share in the ice cream after they have walked in the procession. It is a great way to engage the First Holy Communion children, who can be encouraged to make a small contribution to Down Syndrome Ireland from the gifts they have received.

Families who lovingly accept the difficult trial of a child with special needs are greatly to be admired ... an invaluable witness of faithfulness to the gift of life
(AL, 47)

40. FAMILY ROSARY

Lord teach us to pray
(Lk 11:1)

Many of the elder members of our parish congregations remember the time when each evening the family gathered to pray the Rosary together. Invite a parishioner to design a family Rosary card for your parish and gift one to each family with Rosary beads asking them to begin by saying one decade of the Rosary each evening, Monday to Friday, so completing one of the mysteries each week.

If your parish gathers at the local grotto or shrine to Our Lady in May or October, invite a different family to come and lead the parish Rosary each evening – the family could be parents, grandparents, children, aunts, uncles and cousins together. This is about encouraging family prayer and inviting families to take responsibility for leading the prayer; it can be a good way of catechising the different generations together.

The family is called to join in daily prayer ... and become ever
more fully a temple in which the Spirit dwells
(AL, 29)

41. OFFERTORY PROCESSION

You prepare a table for me
(Ps 23:5)

In our parishes we can often overlook the significance of the offertory procession and the presentation of the gifts of bread and wine for consecration, our giving of what has been produced from the land gifted to us by God.

On some occasions we add other symbols to it that are not gifts to be offered and do not rightly belong in this part of the Mass. If we wish to bring forward symbols to highlight a particular theme for the Mass, they are to be brought forward at the opening procession of the Mass and placed in a significant space in the sanctuary area – not on the altar.

The presentation of the gifts is the giving by the community of the bread and wine to become the Body and Blood of Christ and is a solemn moment during the eucharistic celebration. During the year, as different feasts and other special days are highlighted in our liturgies, the parish community is offered opportunities to invite different families to bring forward these gifts. On other days look to invite different families to be involved in this way. They do not all have to carry something but all can come forward together representing the parish community that gives these gifts for consecration.

On Holy Thursday night or at the Easter Vigil the liturgy lends itself to the preparation of the table for Eucharist. On this occasion you could invite families to bring forward the altar linen and the candles and reverently prepare the altar.

Pope Francis gives us a great example of this practice during his papal Masses. It is almost always families that come forward together, each family bringing one of the offertory gifts.

Emphasis should also be given to the importance of family spirituality, prayer and participation in the Sunday Eucharist
(AL, 223)

42. BLESSING OF THE SCHOOL BAGS

Then he embraced them, laid his hands on them
and gave them his blessing
(Mk 10:16)

The beginning of the new school year comes with much anticipation, expectation and preparation. Take this opportunity to invite all school students and teachers/school staff from your parish to come to Mass on one Sunday in early September. Ask them to bring their school bags with them. Let this be the parish community giving its blessing, encouragement and prayerful support to all who are heading back to school, and include all, whatever school they attend, whether it is in the parish or not.

At the opening of the Mass invite them to join the opening procession while carrying their school bags. As they reach the sanctuary, they leave their school bags in a designated space and return to their seats.

Following the Prayer after Communion, the presider should invite the students/staff to come forward to the sanctuary to pick up their school bags and hold them up high for the blessing.

After the blessing of the school bags and the blessing and dismissal of the Mass they will join the recessional procession to return to their families.

Parishes with large numbers of students may need to adapt this activity. It may not be practical to have them in the opening procession or to leave their bags in the sanctuary during Mass. If this is the case, simply base the opening welcome on the theme and invite students forward following the prayer after Communion with their school bags and proceed with the blessing.

PRAYER AND BLESSING

PRESIDER: The Lord be with you.

ALL: And also with you.

PRESIDER: Let us pray. O God, today we gather to celebrate the beginning of a new school year. It is a day filled with joy and excitement, as well as uncertainty and wonder.

God of knowledge and wisdom, we pray to you for all schools that they may be lively centres for learning, new discovery and the pursuit of goodness.

As students begin this new school year, give them open minds and open hearts to learn and to experience more fully the majesty of the world you have created. May this year be full of promise for them, and for their teachers, as together they experience new beginnings and fresh starts. Enable them to grow in knowledge and wisdom during this school year and all the days of their lives.

Now, O God, we ask you to bless these school bags and all they carry through this year and the students and teachers who carry them. In the name of Jesus Christ who lives and reigns with you and the Holy Spirit, one God, now and forever.

ALL: Amen.

For children are a gift. Each one is unique and irreplaceable
(AL, 170)

43. FIRST DAY AT SCHOOL

Anyone who welcomes this little child in my name
welcomes me
(Lk 9:48)

At the beginning of September each year, families in your parish pass a significant milestone when their children have their first day at school. These are days of change and growth for children and parents alike and they can bring forth many emotions, such as anxiety, loss or fear.

Perhaps host a coffee morning for parents who are bringing their children to your parish school for the first time. It will offer an opportunity to meet other parents and to share in the experience together. You could invite some parents from your parish who have been through this experience in recent years to join in.

This is the caring face of the parish offering a safe space for parents to meet and chat. It is also an opportunity to let parents know that the parish is there for them all through their child's life and not just for sacramental occasions.

Schools do not replace parents, but complement them
(AL, 84)

44. VISITATION OF FAMILIES FOR FIRST HOLY COMMUNION

Martha welcomed him into her house
(Lk 10:38)

Preparation for first Holy Communion offers an opportunity for the parish community to connect with families at a significant moment in their child's life.

Gather a group of parishioners together and, with some training, they can become an outreach team for families with children preparing for first Holy Communion. By arrangement, this team should visit families at home, bringing a small gift, perhaps a holy water font for the home, a candle or prayer card for their prayer space, as well as the good wishes and prayers of the parish community.

During the year there are times of significance in the preparation programme – enrolment, 'Do This in Memory' Masses, first Confession. Invite the team to be present on these occasions so they become familiar faces to both parents and children. Friendships are formed and parishes can grow in many ways through such initiatives.

This is a great form of outreach and reconnection between families and the parish community.

The Church is called to cooperate with parents through suitable pastoral initiatives, assisting them in the fulfilment of their educational mission

(AL, 85)

45. A SNAPSHOT OF PARISH LIFE: WORLD PHOTOGRAPHY DAY

Go out to the whole world; proclaim the Good News
(Mk 16:15)

This is an international day held on 19 August each year when everyone is encouraged to pick up their camera and capture a snapshot of life on that day to be shared on the website www.worldphoto.org.

It also offers some unique opportunities to engage in taking photos of life in our parish communities.

YOU COULD:
- Invite parishioners to take photos on the day and bring them to the church or parish centre to create a display entitled 'Our Parish Today'
- Choose a particular theme and invite parishioners to take photos that speak to the theme for a parish display
- Ask parishioners to search out old photos of life in the parish over the years to share in a display

There are many ways to engage people of all ages in this special day. Make sure you extend the invitation to people in the wider community who do not necessarily attend regularly. It is just one more way to open the door and welcome their participation in parish activities.

The Lord is also with us today, as we seek to practice and pass on the Gospel of the family

(AL, 60)

46. THE ACT OF GIVING: WORLD HOMELESS DAY

*In so far as you did this to one of the least of these brothers
and sisters of mine, you did it to me*
(Mt 25:40)

Every year on 10 October, World Homeless Day is marked across the globe. It is a day to draw attention to homeless people's needs locally and provides opportunities for the parish to get involved in responding to homelessness.

Perhaps organise a collection of scarves, gloves and warm socks to take as a gift from the parish community to one of the many agencies and charities who will distribute them to those in need. At this time of year when the weather is getting colder these items are most welcome and of great benefit.

Another great idea, especially in cities, is to just leave a scarf tied to a tree, lamp post or street sign, with a little note saying, 'A small gift for you, to keep you warm today'. This is especially welcome when the weather gets very cold and it means that anyone who needs it can take it. Once the first scarf is left you will be amazed how many more will be left around for collection by those in need.

To give freely and fully ... is demanded by the Gospel
(AL, 102)

47. PARISH PICNIC

Sit down on the grass; then he took five loaves and the two
fish, raised his eyes to heaven and said the blessing ... they
all ate as much as they wanted
(Mt 14:19–20)

A picnic is a gathering for all ages in the parish, which will see neighbours, friends and strangers coming together to share food. It is always good to choose a significant day in the summer, such as the parish or diocesan feast day, gathering at a local shrine, or one of the feast days of the summer.

Invite everyone to come with a picnic and bring picnic rugs, tables and chairs. Make prior arrangements for entertainment in the form of sports, games, races for the children or even a treasure hunt. You could have face-painting, crafts and other activities, the greater the variety the better. Invite local musicians and choirs to provide musical entertainment so that there is something for everyone.

You could have best dressed lady and gentleman competitions for the adults! Or even the best dressed family!

WHAT WILL MAKE THIS PICNIC DIFFERENT
Begin with a reading from one of the following Gospel stories of Jesus feeding the crowds and then pray grace together before the picnic begins.

GOSPEL STORIES: Mark 6:34–41; Mark 8:1–8; Luke 9:12–17

GRACE BEFORE MEALS

Bless us O Lord and these your gifts which of your bounty we are about to receive through Christ our Lord, Amen.

It also helps to break the routine with a party ... as long as we can celebrate, we are able to rekindle our love ... to colour our daily routine with hope
(AL, 227)

48. FAMILY PRAYER PACK

So you should pray like this ...
(Mt 6:9)

Encouraging family prayer should be an aim of parish pastoral groups. Sometimes families need a little help to get started. Putting together parish family prayer packs and gifting them to families can be helpful. These packs can be gifted to those preparing for sacraments, at Baptisms or when a child starts school.

All you need to begin is a willing group of volunteers who will make bags or boxes to hold the 'tools' for family prayer. The pack can include a candle, a small crucifix, a prayer book, Rosary beads, holy water – anything helpful for family prayer. You could even create your own parish family prayer book as part of this initiative.

Decide who you will gift the packs to, and set aside a day after Mass to distribute them.

There is, of course, no reason why these packs could not be readily available for anyone to purchase (or make a donation for) to use in their own family or to gift to others.

The family is thus the place where parents become their
children's first teachers in the faith. They learn this 'trade',
passing it down from one person to another
(AL, 16)

49. BLESSING OF HOMES

Whatever house you enter, let your first words be,
'Peace to this house'
(Lk 10:5)

Every year new people move into our parishes. Some we will get to know but others will remain strangers.

Why not set up a welcome group that will look out for new people moving into the parish and will call to offer a word of welcome? Perhaps you could have a parish welcome card designed to be given to newcomers.

Your card could offer a blessing for their new home. They don't need to make a decision immediately, but just to know that the offer is there for them. If the offer is accepted, perhaps invite a member of the welcome group who is local to them to join with the parish clergy for the blessing.

Some parishes have prepared welcome packs with a variety of information about the parish, such as Mass times, clergy contacts, pastoral group information and contacts, information on schools, and local community groups and services. This can be a most helpful pack to receive if a newcomer does not know the area at all. A friendly call from a member of the parish community can mean so much to someone who has moved to the area and does not know the locality or the people.

BLESSING OF THE HOME

PRESIDER: Peace be to this house and all who will live here.

My dear friends,
Let us now pray that the Lord will enter this home
and bless it with his presence.
May the lord always be here among you,
deepen your love for each other,
share in your joys,
and comfort you in your sorrows.
May your home be a place of love,
filled with the goodness of the Lord. Amen.

Families and homes go together
(AL, 44)

50. BLESSING OF EXPECTANT PARENTS

Do not be afraid; you have won God's favour.
You are to bear a Son, and you must name him Jesus
(Lk 1:31–32)

The announcement of the coming of a new child into the family always brings great excitement and joy to the parents and to the wider circle of family and friends. Offer a special blessing for parents expecting a child, whether through birth or adoption, on two occasions during the year. This blessing could be offered at a Sunday Eucharist celebration or a special time could be set aside in the evening of a chosen feast day.

For parents the time they spend waiting for the arrival of their child is often filled with anxiety. It can also be an anxious time for the prospective grandparents and other family members. Waiting is never easy and pregnancy can bring sickness, while waiting for adoption can bring its own challenges.

This is an opportunity for the wider parish community of faith to pray especially for these expectant parents and to offer them love and support.

SUGGESTED DAYS OR SEASONS:
25 MARCH – Feast of the Annunciation
21 NOVEMBER – Presentation of the Blessed Virgin Mary
SEASON OF ADVENT – our time of waiting

Make sure your invitation is extended to the wider community, as blessings often draw people to the church who may not usually connect with the faith community on a regular basis.

Ask parishioners to invite neighbours from the locality who are expecting a child to come with them. Sometimes inviting someone to attend with you means more to them and is more encouraging.

PRAYER OF BLESSING

PRESIDER: Today we praise God for the gift of new life that he is giving to this family.

We join in prayer for .... and their child and ask God to protect them.

All glory and praise is yours almighty father,
for you have gifted this family with the joy of a new member.
Open their hearts to embrace this new child.
Let the life in ....'s womb bring us all to experience the mystery of your life
and to know the joy of your presence among us.
We ask this through Christ our Lord. Amen.

Every child growing in the mother's womb is part of the eternal loving plan of God
(AL, 168)

51. CHILDREN'S LITURGY GROUP: SHARING THE WORD OF GOD

Then people brought little children to him
(Mt 19:13)

A separate children's liturgy of the word for Sundays can be a great way to share the word of God with children and involve them in the life of the parish.

You need a group of adults who will lead this initiative. Parents are ideal as this really is about encouraging parents to share the Word of God with their children. They will need encouragement and support as they get started but their investment will bear much fruit in time as they grow in confidence and develop their gifts.

After the penitential rite, the celebrant invites the children to come forward and hands the children's lectionary to one of them. All the children (those who are seven and under) go to a separate room in the church building. (When they begin the 'Do This In Memory' programme for first Holy Communion they should remain in the church.)

Here they listen to the readings adapted for children and are helped by the leaders to understand the message. Explanations can take place through art, music, symbols, etc.

Before the presentation of the gifts they return to the church and show the celebrant what they have been learning about Jesus.

Activity sheets may also be provided for children to take home and parents are encouraged to share again the story and message of the liturgy at home with their children.

Resources:

Katie Thompson, *The Liturgy of the Word with Children*, Suffolk: Kevin Mayhew, 2004.

Faith Map: Resources for Children based on Sunday Readings, Dublin: Redemptorist Publications, 2005.

Bernadette Sweetman, *Our Family Mass: Resources for the Family Sunday Liturgy* (Year A, Year B, Year C), Dublin: Veritas, 2010–2012.

Children's Lectionaries:

Christiane Brusselmans, Paule Freeburg, Edward Matthews, Christopher Walker, *Sunday Book of Readings: The Lectionary Adapted for Children*, Loveland, OH: Treehaus, 2008.

Joan Brown, *Welcome the Word: Celebrating the Liturgy of the Word with Children*, Geoffrey Chapman, 1995.

The Bible also presents the family as the place where children are brought up in the faith.

(AL, 16)

52. PANCAKE PARTY

Blessed is anyone who will share the meal
in the kingdom of God
(Lk 14:15)

Shrove Tuesday or Mardi Gras offers us a wonderful opportunity for a parish gathering of families on the last day before Lent. Invite some parishioners to make pancakes to share with all who come and have your hospitality team on hand to serve tea or coffee. Before the pancakes are served, invite someone to tell the story of why we eat pancakes on this day.

Story of Shrove Tuesday
Shrove Tuesday is the feast day before the season of Lent begins on Ash Wednesday. Traditionally, people would go to Confession on this day and be 'shriven' or absolved of their sins. This is why we call it Shrove Tuesday. Mardi Gras, as it is known in some traditions, means 'fat Tuesday' in French and refers to the eating up of all the foods one is giving up for Lent.

Pancakes are traditionally eaten on this day because they are an easy way of using up the rich foods from the kitchen pantry, such as eggs, milk and sugar, before the forty day lenten fast begins. For Christians the pancakes symbolise the four pillars of the Christian faith, namely, eggs for creation, flour the mainstay of the human diet, salt for wholeness and milk for purity. All of these are used in the making of the pancake. The emphasis of eating plainer, simpler foods in Lent meant that in times past people ate no eggs or dairy products for the duration. Today life has changed and we tend to give up rich sugary foods, such as chocolate or sweets, for Lent.

Alongside the pancake party you could have a pancake race for the cooks. They would run/walk a set distance while tossing the pancake in the pan. This can be great fun for all, those taking part and those watching. For the children, have a variety of toppings to decorate their pancakes.

This is a great after-school activity. After the primary school children are collected from school they can come with parents/grandparents to the pancake party. Some parishes might choose to host the pancake party after the morning weekday Mass.

The spouses ... starting with the simple ordinary things
of life ... can make visible the love with which
Christ loves his Church
(AL, 121)

53. WORLD BOOK DAY: STORYTELLING

He told them many things in parables
(Mt 13:2)

World Book Day happens every year at the beginning of March. It offers an opportunity to engage in storytelling with families. You could ask teenagers to choose Bible stories to come and tell to the younger children as an after-school activity in your parish centre. Make the space attractive to the children and have the teenagers well prepared. After the story time have fruit and juice available for the children.

Alternatively, invite some local celebrities to engage with the community by becoming the storytellers. Let them choose their favourite Bible story and read it for the children.

Christian communities are called to offer support to the
educational mission of families
(AL, 279)

54. FAMILY MEALS TOGETHER

We will celebrate by having a feast
(Lk 15:23)

An important place in each family home is the dinner table where family members come to break bread together and to share the stories of their day. As family life gets busier and less structured due to the work commitments of parents and the increasing number of activities children participate in each week, sitting down together can often become a rare occurrence, yet it is a vital time for families. It should be included in the weekly plan and made a special time when all the family prepare and share a meal together. It is here that we can encourage families to pause as they sit together to give thanks to God for the food, for all who produced and prepared the meal to be shared and for the gift of each person who sits at the table.

Parishes should prepare a prayer card for families to take home with the grace before and after meals on it as a reminder to all to give thanks for what we share.

GRACE BEFORE MEALS

Bless us, O God, as we sit together.
Bless the food we eat today.
Bless the hands that made the food.
Bless us, O God, Amen.

GRACE AFTER MEALS

Thank you, God, for the food we have eaten.
Thank you, God, for all our friends.
Thank you, God, for everything.
Thank you, God, Amen.

Easter Sunday Blessing of the Food

The tradition of blessing food on Easter Sunday can be encouraged by sharing with families the newly blessed Easter water to bless their food and their family as they sit together for their Easter meal. Give them a copy of the prayer of blessing too.

PRAYER OF BLESSING ON EASTER SUNDAY

Lord, as we gather together as family and friends we invite you once again into our lives.
May the hope of your Resurrection colour our days.
May the promise of your spirit working in us light up our lives.
May the love you revealed to us shape our giving.
May the truth in your word guide our journeys,
and may the joy of your kingdom fill our home.
As we gather together on this Easter day to celebrate your glorious Resurrection. We ask you to bless this food we will share and each of us who share together in this time of celebration. Amen.

Sprinkle the food and the family with the holy water

The joy of love experienced by families
is also the joy of the Church
(AL, 1)

55. CELEBRATING THE TALENT IN OUR PARISH

There are many different gifts,
but it is always the same Spirit
(1 Cor 12:4)

Every parish is blessed with many gifted parishioners. Consider hosting a weekend of celebration to showcase the diversity of talents among your parishioners.

Invite craftspeople, knitters, artists, photographers, bakers, woodworkers, sculptors, poets and writers to create something for the event, then host a showcase to display and share the talent and skill in your parish community. The showcase could be closed with a concert, allowing musicians, singers, dancers, comedians and entertainers to come together.

Suitable times for this event are Pentecost, when we celebrate the gifts of the Holy Spirit coming upon the Apostles, around the time of your parish feast day or the time of an anniversary in your parish.

This is a great way of celebrating the people of the community and of revealing hidden talents among them.

We rejoice at the good of others when we see their dignity
and value their abilities and good works
(AL, 109)

APPENDIX FOR PARISHES IN IRELAND

GROW IN LOVE:
PRAYER SERVICES

While they, going out, preached everywhere, the Lord working in them and confirming the word by the signs that accompanied it
(Mk 16:20)

In Ireland the new primary school religious education programme, *Grow in Love*, has been introduced with its inbuilt connections between home, school and parish. The parish now has a golden opportunity to build real and lasting partnerships with the parents and their children.

Each module has a prepared prayer service which could be led by parishioners with the children and their teachers. Parents and grandparents could be invited along too. It is a way of getting to know the families and of them getting to know the parish and its people.

The prayer service might even be held in the parish church occasionally or in the parish centre to encourage families to become more familiar with the parish surroundings and the faith community. A cup of tea might also be offered afterwards to all who gather to pray.

The programme also encourages children to visit the parish church and this could be an opportunity for parishioners to engage with them. Perhaps the sacristan could show the children what is in the sacristy and how they prepare for Mass each day. The altar society members could talk about the vestments and altar linen and how they care for them.

The altar servers might show the younger children how they serve Mass. The priest might then demonstrate how he prepares to celebrate Mass.

Other parishioners could talk about the art in the church, the stained-glass windows, the Stations of the Cross, the statuary and icons in the church. There is so much to see and get to know about our sacred spaces that this might happen over several visits to the church as children progress through the primary school. Allow children to explore and ask questions. This is how they learn and they often teach their parents as they share with them about their day at school and all that they have experienced and learned.

Tell the coming generation the glorious deeds of the Lord, and his might, and the wonders which he has wrought
(AL, 16)

CATHOLIC SCHOOLS WEEK

You are witnesses
(Lk 24:47)

At the end of January each year we celebrate Catholic Schools Week with a different theme and resources prepared. Parishes can use this opportunity to make tangible connections between home, school and parish. Some examples of what is possible are:

- Invite all the schools in your parish to come to one of your weekday celebrations of Mass. Adopt the theme of Catholic Schools Week and invite parents to join for the celebration of this Mass. If your schools are large, perhaps one class from each school could come together for the celebration of Mass.
- On the Sunday invite a representative group from each of the schools in your parish to come to Mass and to participate in the music, opening procession, readings, offertory procession and to prepare a display on the theme of Catholic Schools Week. Invite some of the students to be present to talk to parishioners about the theme and what they have been learning.
- One day during the week is designated as Grandparents' Day, when children invite their grandparents to visit them at school. The parishioners could prepare and lead a prayer session as part of this day in the school, and even prepare a cup of tea for all the grandparents.
- The parish could invite a speaker to come and speak